HELEN EISENBACH is the author of the novel *Loonglow* and the writer and director of *Lesbian Bathhouse*, recently sold out its off-Broadway run. She is the former editor of the magazine *QW* and has contributed to the *New York Times*, *New York* magazine, *The Village Voice*, and other publications. She lives in New York City.

Lesbianism
Made Easy

Helen Eisenbach

A *Virago* Book

Published by Virago Press 1997

First published in the United States by
Crown Publishers, Inc., New York. Member of the
Crown Publishing Group. Random House, Inc.
New York, Toronto, London, Sydney, Auckland
CROWN is a trademark of Crown Publishers, Inc.

Copyright © Helen Eisenbach 1996

A CIP catalogue record for this book is available
from the British Library

ISBN 1 86049 279 7

Typeset in Perpetua by M Rules
Printed and bound in Great Britain by
Clays Ltd, St Ives plc

Virago
A Division of
Little, Brown and Company (UK)
Brettenham House
Lancaster Place
London WC2E 7EN

FOR MAY

Acknowledgements

The author would like to thank:

Lydia Wills, for being personally and professionally sublime; the irrepressible, continually inspiring Michael Denneny; Arthur Eisenbach, for his unique devotion and support; C. I. "Kitten" Hersh, for daily evil and mock love; John Clark, straight man extraordinaire; the indefatigable and blonde Camille Smith; Eric Ashworth, big sweetheart; and May Eisenbach, beloved by many, most particularly her daughter.

Contents

CHAPTER ONE

HOW TO BE HOMOSEXUAL

What Is a Lesbian?

Like many people, you may think you've never met a lesbian. Who could blame you? Unlike male homosexuality, which comes with an easy-to-use ID kit for locating its members professionally (florist, hairdresser, agent, interior designer, marine) or socially (the opera, musicals featuring aging females or male ingenues, any party thrown by Elizabeth Taylor, congressional men's rooms), female homosexuality is a far more complex and intriguing business, rife with confusion and false advertising.

Yet lesbians are all around us, strolling through every walk of life, profession, social class, religious affiliation, and health club, although not yours. How do we know this? Trust us; we do: we can spot a lesbian on a fashion catwalk or Republican fund-raiser, in blinding sunlight or under cover of the darkest night. We can even tell if *you're* a lesbian.

Once you familiarize yourself with our simple yet elaborate system of identifying where lesbians may be found, in fact, you'll be finding them everywhere you turn. Isn't that nice? Female homosexuals may be more of a challenge to spot than male members of the club, but they exist to be spotted in greater numbers than you'd think.

Before we get down to our highly scientific method of lesbian identification, though, let's take a moment to find out a little more about you.

Are You a Lesbian?

<small>The Questionnaire</small>

After sex I often feel (choose one or more):

a. Ashamed
b. Guilty
c. Anxious to be alone
d. Vaguely dissatisfied
e. Like moving just a few of my personal items into my new friend's apartment

If you chose from any or all of answers (a)–(d), all we can say with any certainty is that you were born and/or raised in the United States, very possibly in a Catholic household. If you answered (e), do we even have to say it? You are a lesbian.

When in the presence of Uma Thurman, I usually feel:

a. Warm and/or tingly
b. Slightly faint
c. Hungry
d. All of the above, not to mention *whew!*
e. Other

This is a trick question. Answers (a)–(d) prove nothing except that you're alive. If you chose (e), you're not fooling anyone. There are no other answers.

My favorite color is (choose one or more):

a. Eggshell
b. Mauve

c. Fuchsia
d. Cinnamon
e. Black
f. Purple

If you selected answers (a) through (e), you are a homosexual, though not a lesbian. If you chose (e) and (f), or (f) alone, you are either a lesbian or a fourteen-year-old girl, possibly both.

Often when I see couples kissing in public places, I am overcome with:
a. Disgust
b. Envy
c. Anger
d. A desire to burst into tears

Finding public displays of a sexual nature objectionable may be the result of a lifetime of being denied similar means of self-expression except in dark, tasteful establishments with bouncers named Lou, but more likely, it indicates a belief in the fundamental human right not to have to watch strangers having sex unless money has exchanged hands.

As for displays of simple affection, as opposed to those bordering on public fornication, well, genuine affection is a beautiful thing; in fact, there is far too little evidence of it in the world today, though I can't speak for the Scandinavian countries. Those of you who find yourselves troubled by the sight of such displays of simple affection, whether between homosexuals or heterosexuals, would do well to recognize that such an embittered attitude will only make it more difficult for you to find that special someone meant for you, as soon as you break up with your current girlfriend.

The adjective people use most often to describe me is:
  a. Morose
  b. Playful
  c. Nurturing
  d. Cheerful
  e. Judgmental
  f. Outgoing
  g. Sarcastic
  h. Carefree

If you were torn between answers (a), (c), (e), and (g), you are very likely a lesbian. If you chose any from the remaining group, particularly (h), you are not, though we would like you to consider joining. We realize that those of you who chose (h) have only a very slight chance of entering the fold(s), though plentiful openings remain for those who would like to be male homosexuals.

Every time someone mentions Madonna, I feel:
  a. A craving for raw meat
  b. Like a virgin
  c. Bored and/or nauseated

This question has traditionally been a cornerstone of sexual identity. Unfortunately, it has passed its expiration date.

When I bite into a nice juicy piece of fruit, I feel:
   a.   Satisfied
   b.   Dirty
   c.   Happy
   d.   Tired

There is no explanation for the way you feel.

Clearly, we could continue to ask an infinite or merely endless number of probing, simplistic questions, but as you've no doubt started to suspect, determining sexual identity is a far more subtle and complex matter than you initially realized, and we are starting to get a little tired of making up answers.

Take heart, however. After you have studied the extremely technical parts of the text to follow, you should be far better prepared to determine what, if any, your sexual orientation may be.

Where Do Lesbians Come From?

Some people are born lesbians, some achieve lesbianism, and some have lesbianism thrust upon them.

Perhaps you are not yet clear which, if any, of these categories describes you.

Maybe your life has traveled a path similar to that of a friend of ours – let's call her Mo.* Suppose, like Mo, you knew from the time you were a small, annoying child that all you wanted to do in life was crawl onto the lap of any neighboring female who'd let you, not including Mrs. Lerber, and live there until you died. As you approached adolescence, you felt not the slightest shyness about "tickling" your best friend Susie and eventually you used your skill at wielding a dare to persuade her to try some variations on that special something grown-ups seem to enjoy, until you ultimately got it right.

Fairly early on, your relatives stopped asking whether you'd met a nice boy and sharing their dreams of that big wedding with you in white and scads of children right away. At family gatherings large and small, you've invariably been the person called on whenever a carburetor requires changing or a leaky roof or faucet needs fixing. Basically, you've known where your bread was buttered, to put a delicate spin on it, from pretty much the moment you realized there

* her real name

was bread, though perhaps it took a while longer to realize you could actually eat some.

Do we have to spell it out? *You were born a lesbian.*

Now say the idea of sleeping with women is one that came to you via the assistance of your feminist studies program, like our friend Jane.* Like Jane, you may not have had any physically satisfying sexual experiences, either with women or men, but you've made your decision. After spending time around people of varying genders, you've come to the conclusion that this heterosexuality business is bad, bad news: a system created chiefly to deny women and reward men. It's not that you actually *like* the women with whom you come into contact, but you like what they stand for, and that's what counts. At times, you even secretly find yourself enjoying men in individual doses, despite your efforts to the contrary, but you despise them as a group, and isn't that the most important thing?

As a rule, you're fairly successful in avoiding physical contact with men, and your numerous efforts to achieve it with a woman, any woman, have consistently borne fruit. You are rarely without a significant other, a like-minded female who wears the mate to your earring and nuzzles you in public, if rarely in private, though you actually prefer this arrangement. Anyway, you don't have time to waste on meaningless sex; you're far too busy making sure non-dues-payers, women who don't truly

* *her real name*

deserve lesbian membership, don't slip into the system by accident.

Congratulations. *You have achieved lesbianism.*

The good news is that many people who display the signs of achieved lesbianism (AL) are, in fact, delayed born lesbians (DBL). Unhappily, far too many practitioners of AL are *faux* lesbians who exist merely to clutter up the lesbian pool, get photographed with their artificially inseminated "partners" ("Noah if it's a boy, though we really hope it will be a girl!"), and generally make sure the rest of us don't have any fun.

To determine whether you are an achieved lesbian, simply answer the following question:

I have always felt that the chief purpose of lesbianism is:

a.   Fomenting the destruction of men
b.   Enjoying the construction of women

If you answered (b), you are a lesbian, though not an achieved one. Somehow in your travels, you must have mistakenly stumbled onto the rickety train of achieved lesbianism; jump off *this very minute.*

As for those of you who answered (a) – well, I don't have to say it out loud, do I? You may wish to remain in denial a while longer – all change is hard – but even if you won't let anyone convince *you* you're just a pale, whiny imitation of a maligned minority instead of the real thing, it may eventually dawn on you that you aren't enjoying this lesbian business as much as all the other girls seem to. Honey, even closet heterosexuals have to be true to who and why they are. Go ahead and grow your hair back. You have every right to have a satisfying life, even if you may not succeed in having it as a lesbian.

Perhaps none of these situations strikes a familiar chord. Just take Mary.*

Perhaps, like Mary, you've gone through life with no real complaints: if anyone asked you, you'd have to say that your existence so far has been a fairly contented one. Sure, you've had sex with men, and while you haven't exactly been transported by it, you haven't minded it, either. Possibly the thought of having sex with a woman has occurred to you – this *is* the nineties – or maybe you tried it a long time ago when you were nine and didn't even have breasts, so whether it really counted is anybody's guess – or there was that one time in college for advanced credit. Still, it probably isn't for you, or else it would have happened by now, wouldn't it, the way it's supposed to? I mean, when all is said and done, this whole sex business has never been that major a thing to you. Why does everybody always have to make such a big deal about it?

True, the other day something did happen to alter your perspective. Out of the blue, your old college roommate's twin, or maybe it was the sister of your high school boyfriend, came to town. Naturally, you offered to show her the sights – and she turned out to be, well . . .

* *her real name*

A lesbian.

Not that this bothered you. In fact, you were surprised at how much it didn't bother you. You began to find this fact, and *her*, increasingly fascinating. Could be you even started wondering what it would be like to kiss her, not to mention whatever else lesbians do. (Sure, you saw *Basic Instinct*, but other than the part about not wearing underwear, you're still a little hazy about specifics.)

So by the time you put your friend's sister/ex-wife – let's call her Kay* – on a plane, you couldn't help feeling a lingering sense of disappointment that you didn't find out more about this lesbian stuff after all.

All right, that last part was a lie. In fact, you *did* end up finding out quite a lot about sleeping with women in general and Kay in particular. And not only were you not shocked at how much you enjoyed yourself, you actually had a better time in bed than you've had in as long as you can remember. But that doesn't make you a . . . *lesbian*. Does it?

Or it could be you're like Anita* and nothing like that has ever happened to you; in fact, the thought of having sex with a woman has never entered your head. Lesbians could have existed all around you and you would never have noticed them, not while they were acting lesbian, anyway.

Though at your sorority reunion, your former best friend did tell you she was a lesbian, and, on top of that, the rest of your friends turned out to be pretty much lesbians, too.

* *her real name*

But just because these were your soul mates, your people, does that mean you have to start asking yourself if this says something about you (and if so, what)?

Okay, so maybe you've started looking at women and asking yourself, Do I lust after *her*? Or that one, there? Possibly you've even begun reevaluating your behavior to see if you've been denying some deep hidden truth about your real nature: Is the fact that you love baking muffins with your friend Liz,* for instance, really a substitute for something far lower in cholesterol? Do you go to yard sales so often with your pal Sally* because you like to make unexpected purchases at reduced prices, or is this actually a sign of displaced longing? When you and your friend Carmen* hang out at her place watching bad movies and eating greasy popcorn, is that what you're *really* doing?

Have you been blind?

Not at all. *You've just had lesbianism thrust upon you.*

Don't be alarmed; there are a number of responses you may have to this newfound opportunity – and it *is* an opportunity.

You may, to take one example purely at random, find yourself having sudden inexplicable outbreaks of sex with complete strangers of the female persuasion. Should you decide to broach the topic with various girlfriends – not that kind – you may find yourself truly amazed at how many of them have been there, if you know where I mean, and I think you do.

Conversely, you may tell yourself that whatever sexual

* *her real name*

feelings you experienced were a freak occurrence, nothing that need threaten your long-held sense of who and what you are. You may, like many screen idols and rhythm-and-blues singers, react to your sudden discovery by having as much sex as you possibly can with whatever man you can enlist, though it's pretty certain your enjoyment will be substantially lower than the last time you remember engaging in such acts.

Or, like many of your fellow denizens of the modern age, you may decide to take a reasoned approach to the matter and face the business of self-definition one day at a time. Who's to judge if you seem to be experiencing a growing interest in women as sexual objects and a waning need for men in re same, especially if you don't act on your feelings? As long as you don't go overboard, where's the harm?

On the other hand, you may respond to having lesbianism thrust upon you in a manner that doesn't concern itself with reason so much as instinct, even faith. It may dawn on you that unlike so many unfortunates, you have been shown a path that, should you choose to take it, promises pleasure beyond your wildest imaginings. It may strike you that, as you've already wasted far too much time, you don't want to waste another second before diving headfirst into the fabulous life awaiting you, the life you are extremely fortunate to have discovered, the life of a nonheterosexual female.

I recommend the latter approach.

Perhaps, as is your right as an American, you prefer to remain in denial a little longer. While you're in there, let's take a look at a typical day in the life of an average lesbian.

Lesbianism: The True Story

7:15 A.M. The sandpaper tongue of your cat, Puss, wakes you as the gentle strain of a Viennese boys' choir pipes softly through your bedroom window. Buffy, the chambermaid, comes into your bedroom with a package that has just arrived via courier from your darling Gabrielle, who returns this evening from Milan. You rip it open: Gabrielle has sent expensive lingerie, which she insists Buffy model for you to make certain it meets with your approval.

7:16 A.M. It does.

7:19 A.M. Overcome with loneliness for the old country, where such traditional undergarment modeling is a sacred, if common, ritual, Buffy breaks down. To comfort her, you allow her to make love to you.

8:16 A.M. Buffy joins your chef, Martine, and housegirl, Simone, in feeding you chocolate truffles, bursting ripe fruit, and very strong coffee. M and S suggest additional lingerie modeling to test the sturdiness of the delicate garments.

8:48 A.M. Your approval emerges further enhanced.

8:49 A.M. In the midst of bathing you, Buffy breaks down again, sobbing that you are the best mistress she has ever had and she would do anything for you, including work free for the rest of her life. She begs you not to leave for work, offering to call your office and tell them you have laryngitis. You explain how wrong it would be to ask her to lie over the phone. She lies over the bath mat.

9:30 A.M.–5:30 P.M. *The office. An average day. Coworkers unsuspecting.*

5:50 P.M. *Home at last. Buffy greets you at the door with a message from a reporter who has heard rumors concerning "the lesbian lifestyle." She intends to call on you that evening to do some preliminary investigation.*

5:53 P.M. *You receive a telegram: Gabrielle will be delayed several days. In her stead, she is sending her beautiful young cousin Rafaela, who has never seen the sights. Gabrielle encourages you to show her as many of them as time and energy permit.*

7:14 P.M. *In the backyard, Buffy oversees construction of the new gazebo. The crew introduce themselves as Jade, Dominique, and Vanessa, names that truly suit them. Apologizing for the scantiness of their attire, they assure you that the job will be completed before sunset, as they are known for speed as well as quality. The reporter arrives just as Buffy is serving iced tea and homemade cookies. Buffy offers her a cookie; she eats it, maintaining a professional distance.*

8:19 P.M. *Gazebo accompli. You invite J, D, and V to wash off the by-products of their toil with the hose Buffy is holding semierect and then refresh themselves with a dip in the pool. They explain that they have not brought their bathing suits. You assure them birthday suits will suffice. They display said outfits, leaping into the water. After reasoned investigation of the ensuing frolicking, the reporter joins in, taking special care to hold on to her objectivity.*

10:48 P.M. Group dip concludes satisfactorily, with staff, crew, and reporter lying scattered around the pool, drained. The reporter in particular appears worn-out.

11:02 P.M. Buffy's friend Jan ("Yan"), a masseuse, arrives, looking to try out some new techniques she has learned at the Institute. Undecided whom to choose for her first subject, she suggests the mistress of the house. You demur, explaining the pleasure you receive from the happiness of others. B, J, D, V, and the journalist compete for their place on the table, though the revelry quickly escalates to the point where order no longer seems particularly relevant. Massaging proceeds late into the night.

4:45 A.M. The reporter stumbles into your bedroom, mentioning that she really had not intended to stay this long and, by the way, apologizes for interrupting you. You tell her it is no trouble. Before you can inquire when she intends to file her article or if she would perhaps like to join the three of you, the reporter blurts out that she is having a career crisis: She is uncertain whether she can bring herself to reveal the true story of lesbian lives to a public without the tools to understand and truly appreciate it. You tell her she is welcome to return at any time to continue research gathering until she feels her own understanding is complete. She concedes this may be necessary. Leaving your bedroom, she casts a final wistful glance over her shoulder as if trying to commit the sight to memory. You think of suggesting she take a picture, since you have heard it lasts longer, but as your lips are already occupied, you remain silent, or at least nonverbal. At any rate, there will be no need for pictures, you realize: She will be back. You smile a private smile, returning to matters at hand. The story will remain untold.

Now That You're a Lesbian

First, give yourself and everyone else in the universe an enormous break. Realize that you are incredibly lucky. You could have been born a heterosexual.

You may think, especially if you've been to a movie made in the last ten decades, that being homosexual is at best an inconvenience, at worst something so bad we can't even say it aloud, plus we're tired of hearing it. And it is true that, staying purely on the surface of things, the average onlooker might be persuaded that heterosexuality is the ideal condition, one that enables a person to run the universe, get all the good jobs and special discounts on everything, while homosexuality consigns a person to a lifetime of leaning in darkened doorways squinting out into the sunlight at inaccessible youth and beauty, or standing beside bar stools absorbing cigarette smoke into one's painstakingly chosen clothing until it's time to go home wretched and alone.

This is an illusion. Heterosexuals are, in fact, more miserable than you believe yourself to be at this moment, though it'll pass, you're just going through a rough patch, and many of them – heterosexuals, remember? Try to keep up – never get to experience the journey toward complete self-understanding and personal fulfillment you as a homosexual are pretty much guaranteed once you've attended the orientation meetings. Unless, of course, you're one of the many happy homosexuals who counts her/himself a member of the Republican party, in which case you're far too busy working to pass antigay referenda, "reasoning" with reproductive-health-care providers, forming committees to discuss the military, boycotting television shows with positive portrayals of homosexual characters, deciding the difference between art and perversion, and being photographed at glitzy fund-raisers with your closet-case/prostitute-using husbands and/or alcoholic wives.

Let's return to discussing the ways in which you are fortunate to be born (let's not quibble) homosexual, after a few more pithy slogans even the homosexually impaired would do well to heed. (Note to heterosexual readers: Be sure to delay adopting such maxims until after the obligatory posthomochic waiting period, approximately two minutes after homosexuals finally tire of the idea, three months after first rendering it "hot.") Maxims, for those of you still eating:

- Grab happiness where and when you can find it.
- You exist to experience joy, to delight others, to have a cappuccino now and then but not so often it loses the magic, and to dance by yourself nude (or, if you prefer, naked) with the music turned way up so that your neighbors glare at you in the hallway the next day.
- Remember that life is to be savored. Know that people are put on earth to love and be loved — though not necessarily in that order and, oddly,

rarely at the same time – to eat cookies, and to weep openly at the films of Sharon Stone. Without these experiences, life is meaningless. Less than meaningless.

Female lesbians are especially lucky. There your heterosexual sister is, trudging through life searching for the perfect man who'll spend most of his time with his pals before coming over to have sex with her while she's asleep. Unlike the woman who believes herself consigned to such a dispiriting if cost-effective fate, *you* have been shown another way, possibly at your cousin's wedding. You have discovered the bliss, the joy, the *fun* that life as a nonheterosexual female has to offer.

Warning: If your face is contorting grimly at the mention of the word *fun*, you are exactly the kind of woman who needs to sit down and reevaluate this lesbian thing. Too many of you out there are homosexual for entirely the wrong reasons.

Wrong Reasons to Be a Lesbian

1. Because you hate men

Real lesbians don't hate men; that's what heterosexual women are paid for.

Real lesbians know how to savor the charm and company of those gay males intelligent enough to prefer women for all activities except sodomy, and to shake our heads sadly at our less perceptive gay brothers.* Real lesbians know that gay men, even those who don't remember we're on the same team or actually see us in a room if there are pectorals on display, aren't the enemy. The enemy is joylessness, lack of self-worth, lack of humor, lack of perspective, and a masochistic surrender to the feeling of powerlessness that is somehow part of the female birthright, only partly based in reality and political fact, but we'll get to that when you're lying down.

Real lesbians have no dispute with the heterosexually inclined male, even one who hits on or derides us, because every interaction with a male nonhomosexual is an education – for him. And let's be frank, or at least candid: Who among us does not derive enormous satisfaction from being inarguably in the right?

Here's the thing: You're not a lesbian because you hate men or because you want to force your rage, frustration, and dissatisfaction with the status quo down the throats of everyone in the universe. You're a lesbian because not only do you love women; you even *like* them. If this does not describe you, you shouldn't be a lesbian; you should be a heterosexual man – the benefits are better.

* *Those of you male readers confused by the aforementioned concept should purchase several dozen additional copies of this book immediately for further discussion and/or coffee-table use.*

Wrong Reasons (cont.)

2. Because you hate women

The surprising truth is that many women practicing lesbianism today do so with considerably less tenderness
toward other women than one would expect from studying
the brochure. The reasons for this are complex. Often
women are overcome with (irrational) feelings of inadequacy and a (rational) sense of denied opportunity – two of
the countless fringe benefits of being reared female. Rather
than directing their frustration at inequitable professional
and social codes or the inexplicably continuous distribution
of power to assholes, many females choose a target for
their rage that, being tangible, nearby, and not so physically threatening, can be hit with more accuracy, not to
mention impunity. Who better to blame for the hardships
entailed by living in your skin, after all, than someone
who, while not actually occupying your particular body,
lives in one close enough to it that it might as well be her
fault?

It's easy to see how a woman might reach a breaking
point with her cofemales, lesbian or otherwise. What other
group can be counted on to attack its own members before
ever – if ever – turning its ire on those outsiders who may
actually be guilty? It can be trying to maintain a cheerful
outlook about a person who will never stand up for herself,
whom you can never please, and who won't tell you what
you're doing wrong, though it only seems to take one pina

colada for her to blab it to all her girlfriends, speaking strictly hypothetically, of course.

Contrary to popular opinion and proven fact, however, lesbians are actually luckier than anyone in possession of the various sexual permutations available to humans.

To begin with, we don't have to be men. This may not initially seem to be an advantage, but if you consider the many terrible . . . the many . . . the . . .

We'll get back to that.

Not only do lesbians not have to be men – I *said* I'd get back to the disadvantages, once I think of some – we also get to benefit from the infinite fabulous perks that come with being female. A never-ending supply of gentlemen ever on the lookout to make sure we won't accidentally burn ourselves lighting cigarettes, bang our heads opening doors, or hurt ourselves earning salaries big enough for us to live on springs to mind.

Though lesbians and our heterosexual stepsisters share the same fifteen to fifty-seven years of female life training, those fortunate enough to be nonheterosexual have been shown a secret side exit, granted a reprieve from the permanent effects of such training. If you have learned any of your lessons in girldom, the following should come naturally to you.

My thighs are disgusting.
No, that's okay, you go ahead; I'll stay. Of course I
    don't mind.
Is it me? It's me, isn't it?
Why would anyone want me? I'm so fat.

Call me.

I shouldn't have gotten him/her mad.

But I need you.

What did she expect? She shouldn't have been there in
　　the first place.

He's not so bad.

Unlike your nonhomosexual female, however, your very
existence as an outcast — rebel, if that works better for you —
from the conventions of boy-girldom automatically cancels
your purchase of the above package. Unfortunately, we've
had a few glitches with our publicity, so you may not have
received your flyer; we're still in the process of creating our
full revised-benefits coverage.

Perhaps you know precisely where you stand on the homo
spectrum but remain uncertain whether you wish to climb
aboard. You may have heard a great many things about the
"lifestyle," but which are true and which are mere hyper-
bole? Is the world of the homosexual all roses, or all tragedy
and trauma?

A look at preliminary advantages and disadvantages may
help you come to a final decision.

Lesbianism: Pro and Con

ADVANTAGES	DIS
Forces you to come to terms with yourself as a human being, sexually and emotionally	Universal fear and hatred from total strangers
Automatic bond with others wherever you travel in the world, creating a sort of instant family	Many of whom may be bitchy, humorless, morose, or superficial
Gives you a chance to find out who your true friends are and achieve far more intimacy with people you might otherwise never have really gotten to know	Disownment by family and friends who can't accept you
Vastly improved sex life	Nonexistent sex life
Greatly reduced threat of pregnancy and disease	Continual threat of public drama

Which of these options most appeals to you will determine whether you choose lesbianism or not. Of course, you *do* realize that your sexuality is not a choice; you don't actually choose whom to desire. You may choose to suppress your desire, lie about it, pretend it is unnatural to feel any of the emotions that course through your body every morning, noon, and night, and make the lives of those around you as miserable as you believe your own life deserves to be.

Or you may choose to realize that loving and even desiring another person is a sign not of depravity but of basic humanity. For those of you thinking, just because I have a voice in my head that says, *ooh, her* doesn't mean I have to give in to it, ask yourselves why you were given such feelings in the first place if you weren't meant to express them. If you believe some Higher Power – God, Buddha, Mary, or whatever you might choose to call It – is determining your fate, answer this: why would a just HP be so perverse as to deliberately give you feelings just to make you suffer and expend all your energy trying to extinguish them? Especially when expressing them would make everyone but your husband and present girlfriend so much happier?

Perhaps you still have unanswered questions about the special ups and downs of this life we call "gay." Don't be dismayed. You're in good company.

Beginning Lesbianism:

To be a lesbian, do I have to sleep with women?

Many people, perhaps misled by the examples of such prominent lesbians as [*deleted by publisher*] may feel that actual sexual interaction with women is a minor, even optional, part of being a lesbian. This is an extremely puzzling phenomenon, if you ask me, and unless someone is playing a cruel, cruel game, I think you just did.

The long answer is that societal conditions – never mind, it's too complicated to go into. The short answer is yes. Sex with women – though as a rule not especially easy to obtain, thus the preponderance of – oh, let's not even start. Sex with women is a *mandatory* component of lesbianism.

Those among you who feel in any way distressed or let down by the short answer should perhaps ask yourselves just how serious you are about this lesbian business after all.

To be a lesbian, do I have to sleep only with women?

Circumstances being what they are, too sordid for me to elaborate upon without getting shrill, your confusion is understandable. Even if we were in the business of policing

28

female behavior – and isn't that job best left to those with more experience and appropriate involvement; i.e., men? – one cannot always expect to find undiluted lesbian activity among even pure lesbians.

Don't panic; the occasional slip into the shallow end of the male pool, though not a sign of great discernment or even sanity, does not automatically invalidate your lesbian membership. Like alcoholism, heterosexuality is something from which – the falsely thirst-quenching lure of convention being what it is – one must be in a perpetual state of recovery.

Sleeping only with men, however, is a practice few lesbians have been able to explain or justify convincingly. It is a tradition you would do well to eschew.

I was born with a name so feminine I can't even bring myself to tell you what it is. (All right, Lucinda.) Can I still be a lesbian?

Happily, there is an easy answer to your dilemma. First, to reassure you, of course you can; in fact, your parents have virtually guaranteed your lesbianism merely by saddling you with an emblem of femininity so ripe for parody.

Lesbians over the years who have found themselves in similar straits to yours have established a satisfying, time-honored tradition: that of reducing overly girlie names to monikers of one syllable or less. In your case, the solution is so obvious we're almost embarrassed to say it aloud, though we have before and we will again: Lou.

By the way, any lingering affection you may feel for your given name need not be in vain. The original version does not have to go to waste: Feel free to bestow it on one of your male homosexual friends, for whom it was originally intended anyway.

I have always found women extremely annoying. They always want to talk about their feelings, they rarely spend a tenth of the energy they do on relationships on anything else, like their careers, which if you ask me could use it, and the minute you sleep with them, they act like they own you. Whenever they take their clothes off, though, I seem to lose track of the next several hours. Could I be a lesbian?

Yes. Anyone who does not at one time or another find herself experiencing such frustration with women is either a heterosexual woman, in which case our sympathies, a homosexual man, or the kind of lesbian who ruins it for the rest of us.

Lesbians who believe clinging, obsessive, needy behavior is a sign of devotion rather than neurosis give women everywhere a bad name, and there are more than enough people doing that already. Just the fact that you were spoon-fed girl medicine all through childhood and can whimper, "Call me" in your sleep without even breaking a sweat doesn't mean you shouldn't take a hint from the fact that you're not exactly traditional in other ways. What's lesbianism good for if it doesn't provide an escape valve from conventional social training? (Okay, a few other things.)

Unlike lucky, lucky you, heterosexual women don't have the advantage of mandatory skepticism. What they do have is the benefit of male partners who can be relied upon to counteract neurotic behavior by such helpful responses as not answering the phone, leaving town until it passes, or pretending not to recognize they're being spoken to until the woman speaking either changes the subject or starts in on dinner. Those of us with female partners rarely have the knowledge, training, or forethought to use such tools and would be wracked with guilt if we did.

Still, the fact that you continue to enjoy nude females despite their attendant difficulties is a hopeful sign. Try to concentrate on the positives and behave as if the side effects did not exist.

Hold that thought.

Sudden Interlude

Woman of Your Dreams

SETTING: AN AIRPORT

You stand in the terminal waiting for the updated announcement on how long your flight will be delayed. You glance down the long hallway.

There is a woman walking toward you. You can't take you eyes off her.

After a moment it occurs to you that you've been staring at her openly in a manner that cannot help but make her uncomfortable. When you steal one last look, however, you discover that she is meeting your gaze directly. In fact, she is smiling brazenly at you.

She is approaching you.

This cannot be happening, you tell yourself; still, you seem to be continuing to look quite boldly at her, and not only is she not looking away, she is matching your entranced gaze. Indeed, her smile seems to be growing broader.

"Hi," you blurt out as she approaches and stands inches away from you, beaming right into your eyes.

"Hello," she says, her voice showing a trace of accent.

You blush, hardly able to keep yourself from lowering your eyes.

"Could you be telling me," she says, still smiling, "em, where is this Delta Airline? I am must meeting my husband."

CHAPTER TWO

NAMING NAMES

Naked Vocabulary

Not everyone is cut out to be a lesbian.

In my travels, I see far too few people who truly understand the special responsibilities, the sacred duties, that
come with being the female bearers of the homosexual
torch.

The reason for this is in part a simple matter of terminology. *Nellie*, *fag*, *sissy*, *nancy boy*, *Mary* – these words available
to the male homosexual convey a fun-loving, lyrical quality
sorely absent from the word *lesbian* or its embittered step-
sister, *dyke*.

There is an easy solution to this dilemma. Ask anyone, or
someone who looks exactly like me, and at least one of us
will tell you: Women of the sapphic predilection (a far tastier
term, if you see how this works) have only to announce their
presence via a title that more accurately conveys their true
essence, the myriad bounties of our (or, for you still in
denial, their) natures, and all the fringe benefits of female
homosexuality will come pouring – flooding – in.

At this point, I should take the opportunity to offer the
one appellation guaranteed to empower all who use it, while
changing overnight the public perception of nonheterosexual women as a (w)hole, but I think you know me better
than that.

First let's explore some of the terminology currently
available to today's homosexual, be she male or female.

- *Queer* (*k*-wee-*uhr*)
  Common usage: "What are you, *queer*?"
  Current approved usage: "Oh, Mary, I am *so* over this queer shit, could you *please* take my name off the speakers' list?"

Many people evince strong reactions to the word *queer*, which has both historical resonance and a contemporary application. The label today invokes an image of individuals, neither deliberately male nor female, who sport a preponderance of nose and other strategically placed rings; a defiant absence of hair above the eyebrow; plus the creative sartorial use of a wide variety of white T-shirts, ventilated jeans or cutoff versions thereof, and clunky black footwear designed to evoke the romance and whimsy of Nazi Germany (then, not now).

The word has a certain undeniable power. Bold, brazen, taking no prisoners, *queer* admits not even the remote possibility that its owner could ever be misinformed or misguided about anything. By claiming *queer* as our own, gay people are following a noble tradition. Turning a degrading word on its head, we empower those against whom the term is traditionally wielded while disarming those who wield the epithet – a method that has proven so effective in advancing the plight of African-American black people of color; witness the skillful and empowering use of the word *nigger*, in film, rap songs, drive-by shootings, and video-taped police actions.

Let's take a moment to note the power of language, as demonstrated just then when you weren't looking.

All right, back to *queer*. The word goes some distance toward countering the limp, unattractive image that has haunted homosexuals of yore, though that doesn't make it any easier to say aloud. The oral use of the word *queer* has a side effect of sounding both shrill and bratty, qualities which while helpful when attempting to pick up cute adolescents, are not quite as persuasive during constructive dialogues with, say, the editors of *The New Centurion*.

● *Homo* (Ho!-*mo*)
Common usage: "The place was crawling with homos."
Current approved usage: "Oh, please, they're both *big* homos – I don't care how long they've been married." Alternate: "Let's meet at that fabulous new homo bar that just opened in midtown. Although I don't know what I have to celebrate. If I wasn't such a flaming homo, that job would have been mine."

You may notice that the majority of examples above enhance their *homo* usage via accompanying adjectives. The use of a modifier – as in "major homo," "incorrigible homo," and one I'm told I routinely employ, "raging homo" – serves to indicate to the listener that the application of the word *homo* is intended to be appreciative rather than insulting, though when delivered by a male homosexual, both readings will apply.

If *queer* reads like a tantrum and plays like an invitation to fisticuffs, *homo* is perhaps a little too steeped in whimsy to guarantee optimum success in dealing with potential employers or hardened members of the media (the phrase is redundant). Anyone who doubts the veracity of this maxim should ask herself, though not while riding the subway, how many captains of industry *she* knows who rose through the ranks wielding the word *homo* unless referring to those other than herself. We won't bother asking how many female captains of industry she knows at all, so as not to appear bitter.

- *Fag* (fag-*got*)
  Common usage: "Hey, fag. Come over here and suck my dick."
  Current approved usage: See "Hey . . . dick," above.

The word fag has traditionally been applied to members of the male persuasion, notwithstanding those butch females who can testify to being the lucky recipients of this endearment from less perceptive passersby.

Yet trying times call for trying new things, or at least that's what your therapist told us, which brings us to an important point: Currently existing terms for female homosexuals cannot approach the effectiveness achieved by applying male terms to women.

Traditionally, the usurping of male-identified . . . whatever . . . for female use has been a time-honored feminine prerogative, especially in areas crucial to national security, such as fashion. Only recently, with the advent of RuPaul and her ilk, if *ilk* is the word for it, have the tables been overturned with a vengeance. What is to stop us from applying the same approach to sexual identity?

Transcending conventional methods of self-definition and exploring previously circumscribed modes of expression can be an education in themselves, particularly for your mother. Or, to put it more succinctly, if no less pretentiously: She who casts off her conventional mind-set and tries living life as . . . oh, let's say, a fag, will come away with a radically altered view of the universe in which she lives. (For anecdotal evidence, see "Madonna," Chapter 6.)

The use of terminology traditionally applied to male homosexuals can be a rewarding and enlightening practice for any woman. Don't take my word for it. Go to one of your local establishments and at an appropriate point in the conversation declare yourself a pansy, sissy, fag, top man, or any one of the choices spilling from the cornucopia of faggotry and see what happens. If the ensuing conversation is not far livelier and more hopeful in terms of achieving a true consensus with your fellow humans than a grim, "I'm *gay*, okay?" – well, I'm not going to make idle boasts. Your girlfriend can do that.

Of course, there is no need to limit oneself to preexisting terms. Feel free to try variations on familiar themes, as well. A word like *faggette*, for instance, says, "I like cute girls, but that doesn't mean I'm not committed to overthrowing all forms of oppression while I get my degree in political science with a minor in communications and maybe a little performance art on the side. I live for a good time."

Again, for those of you scowling at the use of the words *cute girls* and *good time*, I'm afraid we've now reached the point where we must ask you to reevaluate the life you have been leading. Go into academia, become productive

members of the American workforce, join the priesthood or
military (don't tell), but give up this lesbian thing. You really
aren't helping.

- *Dyke* (Die!*kuh*)
  Common usage: "Hey, get a load of the dykes!"
  Current approved usage: See "Hey . . . load,"
  above.

Despite a certain amount of bad press concerning the unbri-
dled femininity of those characterized by the word *dyke*,
many who wear the label can be counted on to possess fine
nondesigner qualities. These include: a lack of pretension, a
willingness to speak one's mind, a healthy sense of irony
about the world and one's role in it, an appetite for taking
what life offers – coupled with a keen awareness that life
doesn't offer much or often – an absence of fastidiousness
about sex, and a way with a bawdy anecdote.

When employed by a woman of a certain generation,
dyke must be respected and accepted on its own terms, no
matter how greatly they differ from one's own; you are,
however, permitted a period of unsettlement at finding
yourself being addressed by a woman who resembles your
mother in no way but her need to enlighten you about the
real workings of the world and the bemused, faintly
patronizing tone with which she feels driven to educate
you.

Dyke, when usurped by the young lady of today, has an
unfortunate tendency toward the self-righteous, or at the
very least, the overly self-conscious. When uttered with

more whimsy than belligerence, it has a certain piquant charm, but as the blunt syllable offers fairly little opportunity for shading, one is best advised to employ an alternate.

- *Lesbian* (lezz-*bo*)
  Common usage: "What are you, some kind of *lesbian*?"
  Current approved usage: "Well, she used to be a lesbian. I don't know what *that's* about."

There are women, though I am not among them, who revel in the word *lesbian*, either for its pure historical merit or because of the whiff of sleek Catherine Deneuve-like condescension it offers the outsider or novice. Such women – you know who you are – shudder at the word *dyke* and those who employ or embody it; these women are far less concerned with wearing a label that may be comprehensible or appealing to others as they are in finding one that matches their own tastes and complexions.

There are also females who bravely and dutifully employ the word lesbian out of naïveté about the fact that other choices exist, but anyone in proximity to this chapter no longer has any excuse to continue this practice.

Of course, the word most effective in conveying the true bliss of what you are is:

- *Womanizer* (*Woo*-woo)
  Common usage: "They're a great couple, except that he's a total womanizer."

> Current approved usage: "Darling, I'm not the slightest bit interested in your boyfriend. I'm a womanizer."

There is a true splendor in co-opting terms traditionally unavailable to you as a female. Even more than *fag*, the word *womanizer* has a complexity, a depth, a beauty that cannot fully be explained. However, its very indefinable quality requires your careful deployment of the term, personalizing it for each individual to whom it is being addressed. Even more than the other appellations you may use to explain or announce yourself, *womanizer* mandates your considering your audience's potential reaction, not to mention what result you ultimately wish to achieve. For the casual encounter, try, "You're the kind of woman who makes me glad I'm a womanizer," and let the chips fall where they may. When addressing a woman who seems put off by frivolity or what she will most likely consider your dishonorable intentions, there's nothing stopping you from admitting, "It's true, I am a womanizer . . . still, I suppose the right woman could reform me."

When used on men, whether hetero or homo, *womanizer* tends to suffice without accompaniment or modifier, along with any tasteful equivalents such as babe hound or lady-killer. If females are generally less pleased than threatened by the notion of a woman on the make, the concept has proven especially appetizing to the average male, particularly if the object of a woman's lust is not men in general or himself in particular.

*

Should you find yourself in conversation with a nice middle-aged lady from Des Moines, someone's grandmother, or a woman of indeterminate viewpoint, a specific appellation may not be sufficient to convey the special beauty of who and why you are. Though you are free to select from a vast pool of obliquely creative monikers like *girl's girl* or *bachelor*, your best option may be to eschew a label altogether for a more elaborate string of words, sometimes called a sentence, along the lines of: "I've got nothing against men; I just happen to find women irresistible."

Actually, this declaration is pretty much foolproof whatever the size, shape, or flavor of your audience. "I find women irresistible" is a statement that offers succor, comfort, hope, and amusement to even the most self-loathing or frightened of females. Your new acquaintance may not understand quite what you mean, of course, but that will happen a fair percent of the time anyway, regardless of your actions.

Yet Another Interlude

Woman of Your Dreams II

THE SCENE: A PARK BENCH IN A LARGE METROPOLIS (OPTIONAL)

Several joggers prepare to put their bodies through grueling rituals. You sit on a bench reading. A woman comes and stands by you, stretching for her run. You smile at her, casually, returning to your book.

A young man runs by. The woman looks at him, then you, nodding at his back.

MISS RIGHT: *Great legs, huh?*

YOU: *Not as great as yours.*

MR *(visibly startled): Are you kidding? I hate my legs – they're so fat!*

YOU *(kneeling at her feet): No, see, they're incredibly shapely. [Gently massaging her legs.] You've got to take better care of them, though. Or else find someone to tend to your needs.*

MR: *Uh . . . Look, I really don't go in for [swallowing] you're not one of those . . . lesbians, are you?*

YOU: *Only around really beautiful women.*

Later that day: The woman sharing your cell finally starts to waken, catching sight of you.

"Got a name?" she says.

You concede that you do, reluctantly sharing it with her.

"I'm Sparky." She smiles, revealing her several teeth. "Don't make me come over there, bitch."

CHAPTER THREE

HOW TO PICK UP GIRLS

Female Bonding

A. How to pick up a lesbian

Hee hee hee, HA-HA-HA. Heh.

Excuse me; I thought you were serious.

Try, just try, to get to know a lesbian intimately and you will soon discover the fundamental guiding rule of her existence: She doesn't actually *have* sex. In this, as in everything, heterosexual male porn magazines have grasped the motivating force of female lives with uncanny accuracy.

Single lesbians, or, as they like to call themselves, "bacheloretiquettes," are far too busy perfecting the kind of impenetrably superior seductive appeal that might attract the attention of television newsmagazine programs and talk shows on deadline for in-depth journalistic stories ("Attractive Lesbians: Breaking the Silence") to engage in such messy, tasteless, and ultimately apolitical behavior as interacting nude with other women, especially lesbian ones.

Married lesbians, more thoroughly uncovered later in this chapter, are required to conform to the traditional marital rite of total demise of sexual relations immediately upon transfer of the new mailbox key. There are no exceptions to this rule. (See, Marriage, Lesbian: A Very Special Bond.)

Fortunately, today's lesbian now has a full-time alternative to the sexual act (well, *acts*, if you must know): preparing to be sidebars to magazine articles about homosexual (male) life; posing with headlines displaying variations on the theme "She doesn't look like a lesbian" for public-service announcements, teen magazines, and Sally Jessy Raphael; and changing outfits for the camera to assist in the ongoing, deeply probing media investigation into the high-paying, politically rewarding lesbian lifestyle.

For anyone still undeterred, however, or for those who relish a challenge, there are several approaches that *may* result in the successful seduction of a lesbian. These include:

a. Frequenting lesbian bars with heterosexual boyfriends, who may or may not become too drunk to intrude on any growing feminine intimacies

b. Sending glamorous, rich homosexual boyfriends into lesbian establishments with chemical aids certain to enhance communication and predisposition toward friendliness

Note: Be sure to take several preseduction naps early in the evening so as to be fresh for the festivities when your lesbian is delivered to your fabulous homo boyfriend's glamorous apartment at 4:45 A.M.

Warning: Superficial exposure to suggestions (a) and (b) may lead some readers to conclude that the primary tool in successfully seducing a lesbian, is, oddly enough, a man. This is a fallacy (though true).

In fact, a *fe*male, either one willing to pretend to be your girlfriend or one who may actually believe she *is* your girlfriend, can be a useful aid in snaring your wary lesbian (the phrase is redundant). Large, pedigreed, hideous yet oddly cute dogs named Molly, Mister Boo-man, or Girlfriend may also provide an occasional assist, though this is a highly subjective tool contingent on the personal tastes of your lesbian.

Also invaluable in matters of seduction is the existence of a female who believes *herself* to be the girlfriend of your target lesbian. The optimum time to take advantage of the existence of this extralesbian female accessory is approximately four months after the commitment ceremony or eleven months after the ceremonial unpacking of the van, whichever comes first.

B. How to pick up a straight woman

That's disgusting! It's people like you who give lesbians a bad name. (For more detailed instruction on seducing your heterosexual female, see Section H, page 52.)

C. How to pick up a dyke

Silence is your most effective tool when dealing with the old-world female homosexual. Alcohol helps as well, unless you're dealing with a New Age old-world dyke, in which case knowledge of and empathy regarding the twelve steps of sobriety are essential tools. The best way to pick up a dyke, of course, is a simple, time-honored one: Stay in the vicinity of wherever she is, be it woman's bar or security post, so long that she finally decides she might as well pick you up.

Extremely important note: There is no need to let your dyke in on the fact that you had any active part whatever in her masterful seduction of you. Should you be the kind of woman who believes honesty is the best policy or merely someone incapable of not blabbing whatever's on your mind, you should be prepared for the fact that your dyke will not be as appreciative of your openness as you might expect. Learning that you connived to ensnare her will conflict with her impression of herself as the Big Lesbian in control. Of course, chances are she won't believe you; she may even find it cute that you believe *you* went after *her*.

D. How to handle a flirt

The thing to know when dealing with a practiced flirt of any predilection – and they usually are – is that there's no point fantasizing about all that's going to happen; it already has. The torment you will feel, by the way, will chiefly result not from her teasing but, rather, from your feeling of paralysis in response to it. You may take her flirtation as real and respond in kind, only to be puzzled when the presumably normal escalation from flirting to action will be decidedly onesided – that is, coming only from you. Once you have made a pass and received your rebuff – either explicit or oblique, but obligatory for her ilk – it may seem inappropriate, even rude, for you to continue expressing your interest. Yet it is equally certain that she will continue to tease you, in essence feeling free to come on to you even as your own freedom is curtailed by your desire to take her feelings into consideration.

The problem, of course, is that, being a lady, you've been trained not to ignore how others may feel, even if they may go out of their way to do so for you. The best response to continued teasing – putting aside the lady question, as some of you may have already done instinctively – is to respond as if you have not been forbidden the very activity the flirt seems to be still encouraging you to consider. As there is a decided inequity built into this situation – the flirt has basically covered all her bases while destroying your ability to get to any of yours – you need not feel as hampered as good manners dictate in re responding (that is, not responding) to her quaint remarks about your body or hers.

The first order of the day is to banish your emotional discomfort. There are several ways of accomplishing this. You might try considering the flirt to be someone with whom you once had wild sex, until she revealed herself to be an obsessive psychopath; thus, you can appreciate her physical charms without feeling obliged to think or act upon them warmly. Merely remind yourself she is too insane for you to want to get anywhere near.

Or you could pretend she is an ex-girlfriend with whom you parted gracefully, who is now happily married and thus off-limits due to your essentially decent nature. This does not prevent you from being affectionate with her; it simply prevents you from expecting that affection to lead anywhere.

As she is someone who is far too old not to know who and what she wants, having sex with her would hardly be the fabulous experience her advance press seems to promise, anyway. Indeed, the come-on is probably the only skill she has actually learned.

E. How to pick up a queer gal

Befriend her best boyfriend, be so fabulous that he starts to prefer your company to hers, get him telling so many hilarious stories about you that she starts to get jealous and even hate you; then contrive for you both to be separated from the group at large, don't appear at all pleased to be alone with her, and make a big unexpected pass.

F. How to pick up an activist/actress

Get arrested/in a show with her, the latter preferably one with love scenes, which you will naturally need her help rehearsing. As in cults, constant exposure without hope of release from each other's company can weaken her resistance to your many, many charms.

G. Prelesbians/bisexuals/Cindy Crawford

See Section H, below.

H. How to pick up a straight woman, revisited (you weren't fooling anyone)

The easiest way to pick up a straight woman, which is so obvious you'll be embarrassed you didn't think of it, is to pick up her boyfriend and/or husband. Male heterosexuals, for reasons no one really understands, find the practice of lesbianism – particularly when utilizing their favorite film stars or own personal girlfriends – a particularly appealing way of spending time, second perhaps only to receiving blow jobs. In this, they are united with their homosexual brothers, except for the lesbian part.

Surprisingly many female heterosexuals attached to males are willing to please their boyfriends in this fashion. Of course, there is no reason, other than logic and common decency, to expect the female in question to admit the pleasure she may receive from this hobby of her boyfriend's – particularly if it has ever been a little hobby of hers in those bouncy college days or other times in her excitingly varied life.

Should you not wish to be offended or disappointed by the degree of open enthusiasm your heterosexual displays about having carnal knowledge of with or on you, it pays to adopt a hardened veneer so as to allow certain statements typical of her kind to bounce off your chest without injuring either your self-esteem or any future chances of being called upon for another go at enhancing her sacred relationship.

These statements will usually take the form of: "This isn't really my thing"; "I'm not into women"; "I'm only doing this because I really really love Ted"; and "*Oooh!* That was – I mean, not that I'd ever want to do it again, but *God*, you're . . . sweet."

There are several possible responses to such clearly desperate, if insulting, statements. You may consider a reply along the lines of, "I don't know what it is; I usually find sleeping with women *much* wilder, more uninhibited and multiorgasmic than this!" or a classically simple, "I never want to do *that* again." These insults to your female heterosexual's performance and appeal will, if she's a woman worth having, effectively provoke her to prove to you, and herself, that you very much enjoyed sleeping with her, whatever you may think you're pulling now. No doubt she will even be forced to make you repeat various acts until she's satisfied it's clear to all concerned that while *she* may not choose to enjoy what you're doing together, *you* can't deny that you find it fairly . . . compelling. You should feel free to continue denying your enjoyment, so that she will be forced to call you late into the evenings to reiterate her point, during which time you can explain to her that the phone truly isn't the place for such discussions so why doesn't she come over so you can clear the air once and for all?

Back to her male "companion" and the beauteous inclusive practices therewith.

Once you have completed the obligatory presex warm-up – I always find a group sing-along to a Neil Diamond offering, particularly "I Am, I Said," serves as an extremely effective icebreaker – and the Coke, hummus, and tabouli are gone, it is time to get down to satisfying your partner. (Notice my use of the singular. I'm sure you're perceptive enough to grasp the precise party to whom I am referring.) The male member of your triangle is not your concern in any way, though you may need to get this particular item of business cleared up-front or trouble may ensue. A signed contract may prove helpful.

Start by giving your female heterosexual a massage. This will convey to her that you are not the leering barracuda interested only in your own gratification that she has been led to believe from all the brochures, and it will simulta-neously serve the function of leading her male partner to believe he is, in fact, watching the pornographic movie he has fantasized seeing his entire life up until this very moment.

Once your female partner is completely relaxed, you must take some kind of action to rid yourself, if only temporarily, of her mate; "John, go get the scented oils, please," is particularly useful, especially if in order to obey you he has to leave the apartment and go purchase the product in question, preferably in the next state.

Your goal once John is off on his little errand, by the way, is not to score some brief spasm of heart and muscle but, rather, to share the remarkable transformation of personality and life that is the inevitable result of having sex with a woman, with *you* – the kind of sex she'd barely dreamed was possible but which, now that she's finally experienced it, will make all other sex pale in comparison, rendering her useless to anyone but you for the rest of her days, or at least until you're tired of her.

Perhaps those of you now squirming feel there is something inherently distasteful about attempting to seduce a nonhomosexual female. We are here to disabuse you of that notion. Fairly few humans, female humans in particular, are purely monosexual – that is, either hetero or homo – and there isn't a woman or man alive who wouldn't be in some way delighted to discover there is an alternative to the much-maligned, if debatably winsome, male species. Indeed, by successfully introducing someone to the joys of lesbos, you are showing her a side of the world, herself, and her expanded options that can only enhance her self-esteem and muscle tone, not to mention her disposition, especially after a few more trips around the block with you as personal lesbian tour guide.

Once you realize that showing heterosexual women the options that await them is a remarkably altruistic gesture, you may feel the need for strict adherence to moral codes. Your heterosexual female, by contrast, will expect you to behave in a lustful, predatory fashion, as seen on TV, and will, in fact, be disappointed when you don't.

Go ahead and disappoint her. The most effective way to neutralize the average heterosexual's trepidations about the desire she assumes you feel for her is by *not* making a pass at her, while cheerfully sharing the fact that you're showing your other gal pals things she's only dreamed about, things you'd of course be happy to show her if only she weren't a Montague and you a Capulet.

Should you desire to begin dating your "heterosexual" (whom you may now consider a bisexual or prelesbian, though don't tell *her* that), you must not in any way disparage her relationship with her male companion; in fact, you should encourage it. *You* are not interested in harming the beautiful thing she has found; you are the kind of person who takes love where you can find it, and frankly, the selection just isn't that plentiful for you to turn down a good specimen of female raw material just because she requires some adjustment.

By keeping a cheerful attitude about her heterosexual hobbies, you can relieve her of much of the burden of guilt she is certain to feel; as she is expecting you to judge her for her relationships with men, she will not be able to contain her gratitude and appreciation when you do not.

Eventually, of course, the fact that you are *not* jealous will start to bother her, but depending on how serious you wish your relationship to be, you can always choose an opportune moment to let slip the fact that you want her all to yourself, making sure to take back your immature, possessive declaration immediately on uttering it.

Married women

The time may come when you desire a relationship with a heterosexual not yet ready to consider you a replacement for the mate she already has. Oddly, the best tack to take with someone in this situation is not by saying, "I know you're committed to your husband/boyfriends, but I love you deeply and profoundly and I know we're right for each other," but rather, "We shouldn't do this. We can't do this. We mustn't." For some reason, telling a woman she deserves love and happiness – and, by the way, you're the one to give it to her – is certain to result in failure. Either she will believe that she is unworthy of real bliss or she'll suspect you're the kind of woman who can't be trusted because you've promised it to her. A steady insistence that any happiness is out of the question and a future between you is impossible is really the only foolproof approach; the speed with which both your clothes end up on the floor will astonish you.

Single gals

Should your female be unencumbered by a male companion, wooing her will be a slightly more delicate operation, but persistence is almost sure to win fair maiden's heart, or at least body. Be forewarned, however, that said heart/body will be promptly taken away from you once sunlight streams through your cohabitation bed, remorse and freaking out to follow; and by the way, just to reach that point will require persistence beyond any previous experience you've had with the term.

In dire circumstances, your single gal pal may decide to vent her remorse in a more outer- than inner-directed way, calling all your long-lost relatives to inform them what a degenerate you are, say, or getting married really quickly and then calling you every few days to make sure you aren't exercising your demonic practices on poor unsuspecting heterosexual females other than herself.

Not that having your pure image smeared is necessarily a bad thing. Nothing attracts diligent truth-seekers faster than a sullied reputation. Once you realize that lectures and attempts to reform you are merely smoke screens for a healthy interest in learning precisely and specifically how all those things they suspect you do actually work in real life, being the eye of the storm can be enjoyable.

This is not to make light of the genuine heartache you may feel for whatever woman has brought you to this pass. Your life won't actually be brimming with ecstasy during the periods that all your mutual friends and relatives continue to press for the inside story. On the other hand, you can't expect to be happy all the time, and it is better to risk something than forever regret chances, roads not taken, even if the advantages may not be readily apparent for a few years, or ever.

The long view

Should you find yourself falling inextricably in love with a woman who remains seemingly prelesbian despite your deepening attachment, you should know that while a serious relationship or lifetime commitment is not completely out of the question, it will most likely require a minimum cost of four to five years of seeing her through, in, and out of relationships with men. Carry lots of change.

Note: There is one surefire way to pick up a straight woman: by being a straight woman. Odd though it may appear to the jaded eye, more and more enterprising females today seem to be cheerfully going about having relationships with women, though they don't in any way consider themselves to be lesbians: They just happen to be in love with persons named Julie.

The possibility that straight women may, in fact, be achieving sex with women more easily and often than lesbians bears scrutiny. Perhaps the lack of pressure to achieve a relationship – the very fact that the parties involved cannot imagine anything serious coming of their getting together – is what ultimately brings such a relationship to fruition. The same approach would be recommended for gay women, if only it were possible for them to put the marriage question out of their minds for five minutes, but I can't say I'm optimistic about this prospect.

At any rate, short of a well-executed campaign of deceit, the option of being a straight woman is probably not open to you.

I. Married women and you (homosexual)

Anyone who has been a successful lesbian for any length of time or those novices who have been born with a clue have in their possession the most widely practiced method of girlfriend acquisition: recycling. Most lesbians find their mates, past, present, and future, in the fishbowl of lesbian socializing, demonstrated by the following.

Say you're in a roomful of lesbians. If most of them have not lived or prelived with one another for some period of time before moving on to whoever their girlfriend of the moment happens to be, you're in the wrong room, and these are not lesbians you're drinking cinnamon tea with.

In this, lesbians are distinguished from gay men, who have usually slept with a majority of the men in a gathering without going so far as to consider such quaint practices as "dating," much less cohabiting with any of them. Indeed, in many cases they have not gone to the trouble of learning one another's names, though studies show that knowledge of first names can prove helpful: "That was hot, Rick," provides just enough of a personal touch to achieve a 60 percent greater success rate in getting Rick to repeat the act he's just performed than, "There a bathroom around here, buddy?" Oddly, once they finish the initial stages of trickhood, gay men often cross over into lesbianism, as indicated by the use of actual names versus name stylings: Jeffrey, Kenneth, Robert, and Joey versus Jeff, Ken, Bob, and Chet.

CHAPTER FOUR

THE BISEXUALLY CHALLENGED

How to Pick Up Boys

"*Boys?* We should have expected you'd be another media whore exploiting the current lesbian vogue for your own selfish purposes and completely ignoring the reason lesbianism was invented: the institutionalization of guilt and repression of all sexual desire."

Feel better?

Before we delve into what some might consider a touchy subject, I would like to take the opportunity to reassure those of you anxious about the threat of lesbian slippage, a condition that poses the question, *Is it possible to be a former lesbian?* without ever answering it to anyone's satisfaction. No one, it bears noting, would dream of posing the question about the existence of former male homosexuals, particularly in Hollywood, though you may notice that I happen to be posing it currently. I don't seem to be picking up any of your answers, though.

In my experience, the danger of permanent slippage is vastly overrated. Any woman who has actually experienced the special joy that is homosexual congress, the ultimate transcendence of carnal knowledge of woman – also known as "Madonna" – will for the remainder of her life never again be completely satisfied with the arid, stubbly landscape that is manhood. True, the lesbian nation (the red house, end of the block) faces constant encroachments from male hordes pounding at our walls – excuse me a minute;

63

that's better – but despite the fact that actual sex is most likely to occur if one or more of the participants is not, in fact, female, quantity cedes to quality in the long run, or at least it would if the average woman didn't worry more about how things look to other people than how they feel to her.

Myth: Some women actually prefer sleeping with men.

Reality: Women who, for want of a better roll of the dice, remain forever prelesbian, sleep with men chiefly because they – women, that is – believe their parents and friends will finally approve of them once they find someone who earns over a hundred thousand dollars a year. Obviously, if more women earned bigger salaries, it'd be a whole new ball game.

The primary emotion in dealing with such women, it must be stressed, should be neither anger nor disgust. These creatures are not to be despised. Pitied.

Alternate Reality: Some women may actually enjoy sex with men. There is no scientific explanation for this syndrome. It is possible that these creatures have encountered the rare male life-form that feels something other than disdain for the female body, four of whom have been located in America to date (three in San Jose; the fourth, as everyone knows, has a nice place in Washington). More likely, alas, these females are simply accustomed to going through life with very low expectations.

Where were we?

Oh.

How to pick up boys.

A. Male Homosexuality and You

Perhaps the very existence of a section offering methods for picking up gay boys confuses you even more than the forthcoming inclusion of tips on peaceful coexistence with straight men. *Homosexual*, you may have gone through your life believing, refers to someone who desires sex with someone of the same gender, someone who specifically does not desire sex with the opposite gender, where, when, and if such a gender exists.

You were misinformed.

Homosexuals, contrary to popular myth, are people who, once fully at ease with their own sexuality, insert that sexuality into all aspects of personal interaction, be the lucky recipient of their amorous inclinations busboy or hatcheck girl.

If the thought of lesbians picking up busboys or gay men hatcheck girls strikes you as a contradiction in terms or physical impossibility, you have clearly not spent any time in a primarily homosexual environment. Experience shows that no two homosexuals can be in constant proximity without some form of sex ensuing. Verbal, if not oral.

Before we get into further exploration of the inevitable interactions between you and your homosexual brethren, it should be noted that while you can and will pick up many a male homosexual, *you may not keep him.* Not that either of you will desire this fate. Once your male homosexual accomplishes your complete fashion makeover, utters one last "I've always *liked* women" (or its alternate, "I don't know enough lesbians"), he will grow weary of helping you pick up women and drift off to find twenty or thirty sexual partners of his own.

B. Heterosexual Utility

Here's a little-known truth, except wherever fine adult magazines are sold or in Los Angeles: The vast majority of the sexual attention the average lesbian will receive as she goes about her happy little life will come from heterosexual men.

For handy tips on navigating the perils of being lesbian in a heterosexual male environment, study this realistic scenario:

Holly* sits in a local "neighborhood" (nongay) bar waiting for her friend Claire* (again, any similarity to lesbians you may know is entirely coincidental) to get off work and sweep her off to dinner and a bad video rental.

Several burly, if well-intentioned, heterosexual men attempt to enlist Holly in conversation. Does she:

a. Inform them that as they're members of the oppressive male power structure that keeps all women victimized, she would really appreciate it if they would be so kind as to fuck off, or
b. Share her feelings about Patrick Ewing and the Lakers' chances in the playoffs.

One of the men begins to spin an anecdote in which the word *fag* is uttered. Does Holly:

* *Not her real name – can you believe it?*

a.   Call him a sexist pig, throw her beer in his face, and storm out of the bar, or

b.   Point out sweetly that since she's a fag, he has hurt her feelings, though of course he didn't mean to, and if he simply changes his entire psychological makeup, she won't have to give up on the future of humanity, and yes, she will accept that drink.

Perhaps you cannot yet recognize the advantages to the latter approach. If so, we have a lot of ground to cover, but not in the mood you're in now.

Sidebar

One of the best ways to pick up women, you should be aware, is to frequent promising female-occupied venues with people, women or men, whose company you enjoy. There is nothing more appealing or sexually inviting than the sight of people animatedly enjoying themselves/their friends, sharing an intimacy that the outside witness can't help wishing she shared, albeit without an audience or extras. Lest you take this suggestion as an excuse to use your acquaintances as tools to nab spare booty, you should know that this tactic is effective only when the sentiments you display with your friends are genuine; expecting to nail the woman of your dreams puts a pall on a friendly interaction faster than anything. In fact, this method, while perfect for those nights your one true soul mate happens to wander into the very establishment you're patronizing, inevitably takes a longer time than your short-range plans may require.

Many women witnessing your sociable nature will assume you're either (a) involved romantically with the women with whom you are having a rollicking good time or (b) involved with the men with whom you are having a RGT, though the latter is quite puzzling considering your environs and how obviously lesbian you are. I must admit to being bewildered as to why male-female social units in homosexual bars are always presumed to be heterosexual despite the setting in which they have actively chosen to install themselves. This may explain the warm reception women inevitably get in male bars, and vice versa.

Clearly, the woman who misunderstands the nature of your friendly interactions with men and still approaches you should be commended for not reflexively rejecting you for being straight. (Obviously there is more cause for concern if she hits on you in the presence of what she believes to be your girlfriend, but you're probably looking for just that kind of trouble anyway.)

In fact, you may be surprised at how often female interest will be piqued by your male friends; men, perversely, make remarkable female-baiting accessories. Not only do they make you appear more winsomely female by contrast, they are also guaranteed to keep hounding you until you take action with whatever females are in the immediate vicinity. Even male strangers can be effective tools for intralesbian socialization, truth be told. Heterosexual male strangers in particular are consistently willing to make the effort to speak to strange lesbians – more consistently than when surrounded by heterosexual women, actually, but we're not examining the *male* psyche; if we were, this would be a much shorter book.

That most heterosexual men assume they'll be able to pick up a woman in a lesbian bar, breathtaking in its presumption if sad in its accuracy, has a lesson to teach us: persons who assume they deserve to have women falling all over them will succeed far more often than those who expect females to come to their own independent realizations of one's incredible worth without any helpful pointers from one.

Sample M–F conversation:
MR. WRONG: You sleep with men, too, don't you?
YOU: Do you?
MR W: Of course not!
YOU: Then why should I have to?
MR W: But you're . . . a woman.
YOU: Why don't you sleep with men?
MR W: [Some variation on *Eeuw, gross.*]
YOU: Funny, I feel the same way.

Alternate:
HIM: How about it?
YOU: Thanks, that's a sweet offer, but boys don't do it for me.
HIM: How do you know? You've never had me.
YOU: Don't you remember?*

* *For some reason, the implication that you have had sex with him tends to make the average straight male happier than if he'd had to expend the energy actually to pretend to be interested in satisfying you.*

Such interactions, while charming, soon grow wearisome, but they do serve to occupy your time while you're being ignored by women playing pool, watched critically by women playing pool, addressed coldly by women playing pool, or turned down to dance by women playing pool. And once someone, even a man, has broken the ice by showing you're not only capable of interpersonal exchanges but actually able to attract persons who wish to engage you in them, your further attempts at conversation with females should prove more rewarding.

True, the first woman you approach may not be instantly receptive, but that's to be expected; have your initial exchange, absorb her deer-in-the-headlights reaction, and wander back to safety until your wary lesbian has enough time to decide that perhaps you're not a psychopath and your preliminary words may have been friendly rather than insane.

Not that she will actually go so far as to address you directly; she will merely dart wistful glances your way, glances that say clearly, if pitifully, *You were talking to me a minute ago; why aren't you talking to me now?* For some reason, few women recognize that they possess the ability to initiate repartee; they apparently feel whoever starts the conversational motor is the sole owner of the key and all others have no choice but to sit idling in the car until she gets back into the driver's seat. This inability to climb over from the passenger seat distinguishes them from males, who often assume we either can't drive or don't want to, and if they weren't supposed to drive, they wouldn't have been given penises.

There is another perk sometimes supplied by male heterosexuals: female companions, who, though often heterosexual, can nonetheless prove amusing company. Heterosexual women, assuming they are intelligent and unrepressed, are generally far more open to hearing about your life, hopes, and dreams than strange lesbians. Straight females can also be counted on to recall, suddenly and entertainingly, the first lesbian they ever met, whether that week or when they were twelve. Your enjoyable interaction has the added benefit of awakening your female homosexual audience to several key facts about you: (1) maybe you're not pretending to be a lesbian to poach off their mystique after all; (2) you're not in fact a pathetic, repressed user incapable of recognizing what a closet case you are, and, finally, (3) perhaps you're someone who could conceivably be appealing to women.

The stamp of approval, whether it comes from embittered ex-lovers or complete strangers of the heterosexual variety, carries a market value, sadly, that vastly exceeds the female lesbian's faith in her own judgment.

Performance Piece

What do lesbians do?
Once a month, for no reason at all, they bleed.

You know what I mean. What do they, like, do? With each other?
They put on flowered aprons, make fried chicken, and eat it. With their fingers.

All I want to know is what they do in bed. Is that too much to ask?
The fried chicken part was true; they all do that in bed. Every last one of them.

All right, now you're making fun of me. Why is this so hard for you to answer this one question?
Thank you for asking it; one rarely gets to hear this query posed, other than at gallery openings, baby showers, Halloween parties, and public gatherings featuring persons of the male or female inclination. Assuming you are not a heterosexual man, and thus have been deprived full opportunity to choose from a staggering selection of pornographic films featuring "lesbians," it's extremely brave of you to admit your ignorance on the subject.

You still haven't answered me, though.
It's hard to comprehend how a human being in possession of a body and a mind that understands how it functions cannot imagine what two or more other human beings

might do with each other to incur pleasure. For some reason, the existence of an entire female body in place of one
small penis seems to throw many people into a frenzy of
noncomprehension. This is disheartening. One might
almost suspect that far too many women as well as men are
laboring (and I do mean laboring) under the misapprehen-
sion that the only actual sexual organ is the penis. Nothing
could be further from the truth. The penis is, of course, a
viable sexual organ, but in light of the entire spectrum of
alternative regions on the human body, it is an extremely
minor one.

CHAPTER FIVE

HOW TO HAVE SEX

Practicing Homosexuality

A Brief Warm-up

The following, while widely believed by lesbians to constitute sex, are in reality *not* sex:

1. Talking about Feelings
2. Playing pool
3. Whining
4. Making out with your lover's ex-girlfriend(s) in view of your lover
5. Making out with your ex-lover's current girlfriend in proximity of same
6. Watching tennis, figure-skating, or women's professional golf
7. Whining

Actually, numbers 4 and 5 do constitute sex, or at least a portion thereof, but being both tacky and exceedingly common practices, they do not merit inclusion in a list of confirmed sexual activities. Number 6 can also constitute sex, but I'd rather not go into that.

The following, while widely believed by lesbians not to constitute sex, *are* in reality sex, at least for the next few minutes:

- Utterly silent physical contact, preferably employing skillful use of walls, tables, bar stools, spreadsheets (why do you think they call them – oh, never mind), old girlfriends
- Penetration (calm down)
- Anal sex (I mean it – I don't want to have to tell you again)
- Phone sex

By this we do not mean lengthy conversations about how hurt, frustrated, et cetera, her behavior the other night made you feel. No. In order to constitute phone sex, conversations must employ at least one of the following in a nondomestic context:

a. Take that off
b. *Ooh*
c. How does that feel?
d. Don't stop
e. Faster
f. I thought *you* called the caterer (optional)
g. Put that on
h. Now, don't move at all
i. I *said*, don't move
j. *Oh God*
k. Shit, that's my Call Waiting. I'm not going to answer it; they'll go away – what if it's Pam? I'm supposed to get the keys to feed her cats while she and Kay are in Jamaica.

Why

Most of you reading this have too many inhibitions, pro-hibitions, and fears about sex. Those of you born or, better yet, raised in Europe naturally have the rest of us at a disad-vantage, but there is no reason the majority of us have to suffer for a sheer accident of geography. All of us may learn from the examples of those who have overcome traditional phobias about the erotic component of life.

Taking the male homosexual model might be helpful, if we females were able to stand around in fast-food sex joints and finish ourselves and others off without mussing a hair, but unfortunately and/or fortunately, female sexuality is a far less localized, fetishized, and simplistic thing. Actually, male sexuality is far less simplistic than the rudimentary mechanism would indicate, but we're not here to delve into the misunderstandings prevalent in male sexual congress; there are already plenty of gabby boy writers churning out sex manuals in the guise of tasteful fiction who are free to whine about – excuse me "analyze" – the errors in percep-tion regarding male sexuality. Though it might prove difficult to find a male homosexual willing and able to crit-icize other homosexual men. That was an example of what we call "sarcasm."

The fact is, far too many women grow up as successfully trained and socialized – some might suggest brainwashed – members of American society. Also known as "good girls," they form an enormous cult whose members too often remain ignorant of their sexual needs and desires, guilty about those desires that break through the seal of "he won't buy the cow" training, and certain that fulfilling them in actual sex is evil. There are socially sanctioned methods of making sex acceptable, of course, but these seem limited to talking about it incessantly afterward, ascribing deeper emotions than actually existed at the time, or chasing someone who isn't interested for as long as one is allowed to remain in the same city without temporary restraining orders and then paying little attention to the actual desires of both participants when sex is initiated after the chasee has given up in exhaustion.

How to Have Sex

How to Have Sex

DO'S AND DON'TS

DO HAVE SEX	DON'T DO IT
Frequently	With your father's new wife
For the sheer fun of it	With someone you don't like *that way*
Affectionately	With your sister's girlfriend
With someone you strongly desire	With someone whose politics or taste in music offends you
Imaginatively	With your therapist/accountant/couples counselor/biographer
With someone who pays attention to your responses	With someone whose voice annoys you
With someone you have a great time hanging out with	With a man
Because you're feeling happy	Because you're lonely or restless
Because you're on vacation	With your brother's girlfriend/best friend's daughter/best friend

When

There are two preferred ways of having sex of which you should be aware:

1. Have it immediately, before you know much more about your partner than her name, if that, or
2. Putting it off as long as humanly possible, until you both can't stand waiting another minute.

The second method, often confused with "friendship," is the most commonly practiced in the lesbian community, though far too many women never actually succeed in getting to the consummation portion of the sex. As anyone who's ever been female knows, it's far easier to wait until she makes a pass at you, even if that means waiting forever, than to risk rejection, ugly gossip, or actual sex.

Despite the many temptations to be a sexual coward that are routinely thrown in a gal's path, it is your duty as a modern female to break through your fears and self-doubt, to suppress your feelings of inferiority long enough for you to stammer out how attracted you are to someone. Silent action is preferable to stammering, of course, but it can be far more difficult – or impossible – to achieve.

The first method – immediate sexual action before the exchange of intimacies, such as the year she bought her Jeep or the individual motivations for each of her tattoos – should be undertaken only with the appropriate preparation. Study the following examples:

Wrong: I . . . I really . . . God, this is so – do you think maybe – you're probably busy, but – and I doubt you'd even want to, but do you think some time you might, you know, want to go out? On a date? Well, not like a *date* date, not if you don't want to – I mean, we could just have coffee. Talk. You don't have to if you're busy. It's probably not a good time.

Right: What's a beautiful woman like you doing standing around when you could be experiencing unbelievable ecstasy back at my place?

Some of you may not immediately see the distinction between these two approaches, other than the fact that the first one definitely seems doable and the second, no way. You will discover, however, that brazenness becomes far easier with practice; once you take your first step down the road to contemporary wild womanhood, there's no turning back. True, you are more likely to be greeted with stares of incredulity and shock executing the latter approach than the former, but that's no reason to be fainthearted.

Where

Human flesh, though this will come as a shock to many of you, is a source of pleasure not necessarily localized in those specific areas that will be known to any follower of pornographic films or romantic movies, except those made in the United States. Think of the complete body as an erogenous zone. Certain areas not always given full consideration in erotic discussion can actually be exceedingly promising locales for mining pleasure: ribcages, fingertips, backs of knees, napes of necks, navels. Nor should those areas generally considered erotic be treated like a limited menu with only a few select items from which you are obliged to order. The entire human unit, as you no doubt recall from that book you snuck from your parents' drawer when you were nine, is a veritable cornucopia of delight. If treated like a new piece of machinery to be investigated to see what makes it work, the results can be far more satisfying than if one approaches it by pulling buttons for the sole purpose of seeing if a siren goes off or the motor starts right up, though I'm getting a little dizzy from mixing these metaphors.

Though many of you have survived the joyous period known as "the teen years," when everything good that can happen to your body, soul, and personality is sure to befall you, you may still be living with its consequences in adulthood. In many ways, American sexuality is stalled at adolescence; too often we view sex through juvenile eyes: this is the goal; these are the games to play to achieve it. Even homosexual Americans can be affected by pervasive notions of the ways people – men and women – are "supposed" to have sex. Females of the lesbian stripe, for instance, often sleep with men during adolescence to prove to themselves that they are "normal," and these interactions can leave a residue with even those partners who bear no external similarity to boys. Happily, thanks to all the helpful pamphlets being distributed these days at schools and churches, the number of lesbians who recognize their sexual desire early and feel no need to suppress or deny it is growing.

Bizarre as it may seem, despite the fact that sex between two women often does not entail anything to do with a penis, women nonetheless sometimes behave as if they were still, in fact, having sex with men, by which I mean business rarely ventures outside a limited program and gets under way briskly rather than languidly, as is in many ways more natural to a female's sexual being.

This is not to suggest that all sex between women need be languid or gentle, which will come as a shock to many heterosexuals, but merely that the sensual part of being sexual is invariably undeveloped in the American psyche, and it is high time to develop it.

How

Unlike men, who have all that early training in public displays of nudity and mandatory penis comparison, women have years of furtive bodily discomfort to draw upon when considering employment of said bodies for sexual use. There is a simple solution to whatever damage this early training may have done to you: realize that it serves no function whatever – it doesn't win you fortune or fame, and, in fact, it doesn't make anyone think any better of you; pretend it has been surgically removed without your knowledge or consent. Should you find yourself experiencing recurring symptoms from those early lessons, just remind yourself that you are in the grip of a purely phantom pain; there is no way it can possibly be real. Repeat after me: YOU HAD THE INGRAINED BAD TRAINING SURGICALLY REMOVED. Through no fault of your own.

How (A Closer Look)

Think of another woman's body as a strange, beautiful, and exotic island on which you happen to have miraculously landed. The only thing you have to do, though *have to* really isn't the right state of mind for the junket on which you're about to embark, is take your time exploring the terrain, doing whatever little things you find enjoyable, though don't forget to be mindful of weather conditions and possible turbulence. Remember, you're on vacation. Too often we rush through the act of love as if to make up for all those years everyone else was getting to ram their tongues down one another's throat in movie theaters just to prove they could – and by the way, you couldn't.

The human body is a wondrous thing, even hers; if you treat each corner of the brave new land you've washed up on as if it will yield pleasures heretofore unanticipated, it will likely do just that. Of course, as on any vacation, distractions from the more serious matters of the day are crucial; anytime a feeling of habit, obligation, or rote sinks in, considerable pleasure flies out the window.

It can be quite rewarding to pretend you're somewhere other than where you are, performing activities quite different from those in which you are actually engaged. Sometimes your environment (as she likes to be called) feels a certain pressure to behave a certain way, a pressure you can remove by playfully pretending you and she are not in the process of having sex, but rather, oh, chatting about stress and skin care. Keep your focus casual, if ever-present. Don't go to extremes, of course; you don't want your island to fall off into the ocean. Pretend to be distracted; don't actually *be* it.

The sexual act has been somewhat devalued by the frequency with which we, by which I mean you, attempt to achieve it without regard to spiritual, emotional, and especially compelling physical concerns. Should you not expect the lay of the land to yield fascinating discoveries as you descend upon it (or ascend, as the case may be), you should probably not be making the trip at all.

Inner Beauty

One of the great rewards of lesbianism, among the many too numerous to elaborate upon, is that it is possible to go to bed with someone and feel more beautiful naked than clothed, more desirable than you had any expectation of feeling after being weaned on a diet of American standards in silicone and femininity.

Though as females we are unusually well trained in finding every conceivable fault with our own bodies, the odd thing is that we often are considerably more forgiving when it comes to the imperfections of others, able to see flaws as merely insignificant parts of a delightful whole. Though traditionally male children are not raised to fall for the inner woman (or as the case may be, man) and thus rarely attach themselves to nice old broads with big bucks or scintillating creatures with no external gloss, we females often choose partners whose charms are not instantly apparent. (Actually, we often choose mates whose charms never become apparent, at least to others, but that's a problem too big to tackle here, and not nearly frivolous enough for the purpose of our discussion.) As we have proven ourselves capable of not being hemmed in by superficial concerns when they involve the bodies of others, we should ask ourselves, *Why shouldn't we be able to perform the same feat with our own?*

The fact is, all human beings, with the possible exception of Paulina Porizkova, though she would no doubt contradict me, are born with some sort of physical imperfection. Most of us can, without too much effort, cite at least one physical attribute we would like to change; otherwise, plastic surgeons wouldn't make such a nice living, thank you.

The situation is more dire than one might think. The actress Michelle Pfeiffer, for instance, responded to praise for her breakout film role as a gorgeous, embittered prostitute who finds fame and fortune rolling atop a grand piano in the film *The Fabulous Baker Boys* by pointing out what was wrong with her face, body, and anyone insane enough to think she was anything but a goofy tomboy. The lesson to be learned from this – even without asking other famous beauties, or Julia Roberts, after their breakout roles as prostitutes, what they think of themselves – is that if *Michelle Pfeiffer* has a problem with the way she looks, there's really no point expecting any female not to rattle off a list of physical failings to anyone foolish enough to compliment her.

The only remedy for this condition is to ask yourself if your body provides you pleasure. If so, regardless of how it looks, you should love and appreciate it; enabling you to feel happiness, physical transportment, and ecstasy is the best thing a body can do for you. Isn't it time you let it off the hook for however it may make your heart sink when you catch a glimpse of it in cruelly lit department-store mirrors?

Appetizers

Humans of all persuasions share one area of sexual inter-action that is of primary importance, whether lesbian or otherwise: kissing. Too often the joy of this practice gets lost in the general scramble to achieve the ultimate goal in the game of love, but kissing is an incomparable goal in and of itself.

Sadly, few lesbians grow up with the opportunity granted our nonlesbian peers — that is, to be denied any sanctioned public sexual acts outside the initial gropings known as fore-play or "sexual harassment." There is a decided advantage to being encouraged to act out one's hormonal impulses up to a point only: the safety net provided allows one to develop an appreciation for the finer delicacies of "everything but" without concern for anything but the immediate sensation. Were teenaged girls allowed to engage in such badinage with each other at movie theaters and on park benches like boy-girl couples, there would be no need for heterosexual sex.

Adults are free to relive this aspect of their teens, of course, by performing acts generally known as "teasing," though this activity has been given a fairly bad name. Were the practitioners of this method of communication able to pass out instructions informing those with whom they wished to toy that whatever cowardly impulses might pre-vent them from finishing what they were starting, they nonetheless would like to pursue a mutual enjoyment of the means, if not the end, there would be a lot fewer irritated persons roaming the earth.

Fantasy

Fantasies can be very useful to spice up a limp sexual relationship or enhance one that (you should be so lucky) years of familiarity have drained of all intensity and mystery until the end result is closer to suet pudding than to multiple-layer chocolate-fruit-nut surprise. The practicing homosexual should be forewarned that use of the actual names of past girlfriends or present film stars can be an incitement to violence rather than passion. Also, there is a danger of ruining the purity of the vanilla sexual encounter with too much excitement, which can never be recaptured past the first five or six hundred uses or the batteries wear out.

Three-Letter Word

It is the rare woman who goes through life without at any point running into an asshole, but too few acknowledge the ones closer to home, as it were, and any possible gratification that may be attained therein (or therefrom, but let's not get clinical). Those of you afraid I'm actually going to get specific have no need to get squeamish; allow me simply to point out that in some cultures the ability to allow someone to break new ground, as it were, is a sign of sexual health. If you're holding too tightly to this particular facet of your virginity – and isn't it nice we gals have so many different kinds to lose! – it's time to stop exerting so much control over yourself and give someone who knows what she's doing a chance.

Four-Letter Word

Love, of course, may be a part of sexual activity, but the two are completely separate entities. Though sex with love cannot be recommended too highly, few people in the real world can locate, much less secure, it permanently, and it's far better to acknowledge this winning combo as something to strive for than to misrepresent an unrelated activity as actually being said combo.

Meanwhile, while you're waiting, sex without love may be an entirely pleasurable act, one that is completely justified in and of itself, which brings us way back to our first category of sapphic sexual activity. Too many women have instituted a junior camp school of approaching sex, which is to say, holding hands and being best buddies as the purest form of union between two people. Purity as an admirable goal, while a fine motivating factor for fifties and nineties sitcoms, is a dangerously wrong-headed notion when non-celluloid, and especially lesbian, humans are involved. Those of you who believe sex is nasty, dirty, or inferior to loving friendship should talk to those of your sisters who managed to discover the real point of Girl Scout camp, and we aren't talking merit badges.

Love Games

S&M

In today's market, there are two primary methods of sexual activity currently prevalent among lesbians. These are:

1. Nurturing
2. Dressing in black, leather, or black leather and throwing major attitude

These methods are unacceptable. Less than unacceptable.

In many cases, the existence of the second practice can be directly traced to resultant frustration and disgust at the prevalence of the first, which some might consider a hopeful, even positive, development, or at least a step in the right direction. Sweet though this notion is, it should not stop us from putting both methods under grueling scrutiny.

Let's start with the second category, chiefly because if we don't follow our chapter headings, you'll get unruly.

Ready?

In recent times, the quaint notion that sex is about power, not pleasure, has gained significant currency, as evidenced by the many helpful primers available on the market that assure unsuspecting readers, and you, how healthy it is for them — you — to express them/yourself in terms of the power vector in human activity.

No one would dispute that we live in a world in which abuse of power runs rampant, and no one except all males under and over twenty-five and far too many women would argue that these abuses are practiced in somewhat dispro-portionate amounts upon females, regardless of sexual orientation or hairstyle.

What these books — which, by the way, I've read, though I haven't always gotten to the end, or past the table of con-tents — fail to mention is that channeling your anger, whether at being abused by society at large or your boss in particular, toward a specific female target doesn't do much to enhance the plight of humans, female or male, in the uni-verse. Incidentally, I'd also be curious to know, just for fun, how the average American would react to the suggestion that it is healthy to terrorize *male* sexual partners to express one's newly empowered nature in a dog-eat-dog world, bearing in mind that the publishers of *Gent* and *Hustler* are not the average American.

The aspect most disheartening about so-called S&M sex-ual "play" between women, other than the rarely acknowledged fact that it legitimizes behavior that would be severely complained about if enacted by men (upon women), is the utter absence of sensuality. A rope burn may generate heat, but it's not the sort that really lingers satisfactorily. Certainly there are and will always be people who can find sexual release in the enactment of fantasies of degradation, but why go hunting for what society so plentifully supplies free of charge?

Of course, as I've said before and no doubt will again, though I'm not promising anything, everyone has the right to find sexual pleasure however she sees fit, as long as no animals are tortured, though why this rarely seems to apply to human animals has never been satisfactorily explained. No one can say I'm not all for diversity and imaginative sexual interaction, at least not to my face.

Yet it is a sad indication of the lengths to which women will go to reinforce the negative images we've been trained to accept as our destiny that so many lesbians respond to being considered outcasts by ignoring the true guilt-free pleasures of sensual bliss, focusing instead on the kind of behavior whose chief characteristic is the ability to shock innocent tourists who stumble across them. Sexual activity that achieves its purest realization as an instrument of offense and shock for an audience will always be vastly inferior to that which takes as its chief goal the prolonged sensory gratification of two or more people involved. All right, one or more.

For those who don't receive enough sadomasochistic thrills simply by being female in any city in the United States, the corporate world at large, or certain department stores during major clearance seasons, the least you can do is display a little ingenuity in your gamesmanship. After all, if you're going to be transgressive, shouldn't you be infusing some fresh blood – sorry to put it so delicately – into traditions that have been recycled for altogether too long?

For those of you determined to find the lure of S *or* M irresistible, the time has come to update the timeworn altar boy–priest dynamic with roles that more accurately reflect the richly varied experiences of today's woman. Consider these alternatives:

First Lady/"Friendly" journalist
Talk-show hostess/Sullen pregnant teen
Oscar-winning actress/Female stalker "fan"
Republican socialite/Whoopi Goldberg
Former child actress/Substance-abuse counselor
Supermodel/Roseanne
Religious cult member/Attorney General
Amish housewife/Riot grrl
Safe-sex poster girl/Pregnant antiabortion protester
High-profile district attorney/Recovered-memory expert
Cheerleader/Camille Paglia
Gynecologist/Madonna
Stewardess/Camille Paglia
Anyone (except Madonna)/Camille Paglia

Twenty Questions

Lesbianism Made Fashionable

THE SCENE: "Lesbian Night" at a chic downtown bar/restaurant. The room is overflowing with women speaking in accents, which is how you know it's chic, and the only person who approaches you is a heterosexual man, which is how you know it's lesbian night. He hastens to explain that he is there out of sisterhood: to make a positive statement of support for you and your beautiful, exciting lifestyle. He is eager to learn as much as he can about this fascinating world in which you live, and comfortable enough with you, for some reason, to proceed immediately with furthering his education.

1. *Do you hate men?*

2. *Have you ever slept with a man?**

3. *When did you first know you were gay?*

4. *What attracts you to women? Is it more emotional than sexual?*

5. *Do you have a girlfriend?*

6. *Have you and your girlfriend ever had sex with a guy?*

---

* Those who have never met a straight man will find it curious that the first questions he will invariably ask about lesbianism have surprisingly little to do with women.

7.   *Are you attracted to anyone here?*

8.   *What's your favorite part of a woman's body?*

9.   *Do you like her ass? She has a nice ass, doesn't she?*

10.   *How can gay men put their dicks in each other's butts?*

11.   *I've got nothing against lesbians; I think two women together is a beautiful thing.*

12.   *I couldn't imagine sex with a man. No way. But I can understand what a woman would see in another woman.*

13.   *Where do you meet women?*

14.   *Do you usually go to places like this?*

15.   *Have you ever slept with a woman you didn't know?*

16.   *Don't you miss sex with a penis?*

17.   *What do you . . . you know . . . do?*

18.   *Have you ever been in a long-term relationship with a woman?*

19.   *Would you and your girlfriend ever have sex with a man?*

20.   *What about if I just . . . watched?*

Love Games II

Girls will be boys

In recent years, there has been a resurgence of the once-obligatory practice of butch-femme, whether out of genuine enjoyment, whimsy, or to facilitate an easy-to-use, cash-and-carry sexual relationship for those too timid to come up with a personalized approach to sexual encounters with each individual female with whom they come in contact. I'm not sure *contact* is the word I'm looking for.

There has been a fairly irrational response to this practice, as if the topic under discussion were military encroachment into tiny island nations that pop into American consciousness whenever needed to bolster our floundering sense of invincibility. Like variously colored ribbons or high-volume "reasoning" with those who might not believe every one of life's little crises calls for an armed response, butch-femme comes with its own emblems and openness to free debate. Practitioners of both forms of all-American self-expression sometimes act as if all that is involved is the proud restoration of a historical tenet, with a dash of self-empowerment and a public assertion that we can get the job done (publicity to the contrary notwithstanding) thrown in for good measure. Where lesbians are concerned, of course, the job under discussion is the making of love rather than war. Some permutation thereof, anyway.

Warning: In no way should it be assumed that I am questioning the fabulousness of any lesbian practice(s), up to and

99

including the wielding of butch-femme among members. Having read the charter, I am fully aware that anything lesbians decide to do in theory or as a group – as opposed to individually, one lesbian at a time – is and must be completely invulnerable to criticism. If you'd attended the meeting at which this was decided, after the votes were tallied again that second time, you, too, would have learned that whatever women decide to do, regardless of the patriarchy and all barbaric rules learned under its employ, is automatically and incontrovertibly superior to any suggested alternative.

Like every system of checks and balances, of course, there are assets to assigning roles for specific human beings. Women who considered their options in the 1950s, for instance, no doubt found their burdens vastly lightened by being spared the anxiety of making any choices about the future other than which room in the house to vacuum first. Yet there are undeniable problems with fitting the multiple facets of human nature into neat slots. This applies to the passive wallowing and/or naïve indulgence in the present day of what in the past was for many a limiting series of behaviors, one brought about not because of joyous exultation in eroticism but because society mandated against homosexual liberties in particular and unfettered sexual expression in general. If you think this doesn't still apply to sex in the present day, we encourage you to think again, and we don't encourage lightly.

No one would deny that the world can be a confusing, vast, difficult place; if I did, you'd throw the book across the room, and your roommate would complain. Certainly for those lacking imagination, it must be comforting to have one's sexual persona – indeed, perhaps one's entire personality – spelled out simply and clearly so as to avoid such confusion as happens in the everyday interaction with humans who don't necessarily believe every aspect of life can or should be predicted, categorized, or neatly compartmentalized.

No one could deny that life would be more easily managed if the many unknowns of daily existence were eliminated. Yet while this might be advisable when dealing with the IRS, late-night strolls into deserted areas, bank-card transactions, and the regulation of graduate fellowships, those facets of life involving passion and human physiognomy can actually benefit from containing elements not fully known to the participants, despite fear of random unknown occurrences.

Unknown occurrences, it must be pointed out, are the very stuff that makes life exciting, and by life, we mean of course sex. Such occurrences happen anyway, whether you want them to or not. Why fear them to the degree that you try to mute the very essence of human existence – that is, the fundamental mysterious unknowability of the human psyche? Butch-femme attempts to quantify what is and should be an ultimately unquantifiable property, human sexual invention and identity.

Of course, if you wish to lead your sex life in a fashion whose chief purpose is to render homosexuality easy to understand for heterosexuals – at least those whose sexual IQ has never progressed past the question, *Which one of you is the man?* – that choice is entirely yours. It is not my place to tell you what you should or do find erotic; all people, be they card-carrying members of the ACLU or gym teachers, have certain things that move, delight, and tantalize them more than others. I am merely suggesting that rather than think of sexual behavior as a fast-food costume drama you're on the verge of memorizing your lines for if you could only get a little more rehearsal time, you might consider approaching it as a vastly less portable, less comprehensible, yet more comprehensive method of going through life. Limiting yourself to a fraction of the possibilities or permutations available to you is like reading the same book over and over because you know which passages are going to make you laugh and how the story comes out in the end. Actually, that doesn't sound so bad.

Many people in the world, not all of them Republican, would feel more secure in life if there was no bisexuality, if people of all inclinations and genders felt strictly monogamous in their sexual desires, if all male and female human beings were not in reality comprised of both masculine and feminine traits, particularly fundamentalist preachers. By the same token, many women seem to need the structure of a limited sex role to feel secure in their lesbian identity. It is almost as if once they have finally resigned themselves to losing the grand prize in the "rich husband for self-worth and societal approval" sweepstakes, they must seek out a convention to replace the discarded one, thus reassuring themselves that at least they're capable of following *some* rules. That so many women race to embrace restrictive behaviors should not be surprising in light of the quintessentially female trait to seek out behaviors that confirm one's own worthlessness while enabling one to speak at length about such worthlessness to anyone who will listen.

That is not to say that there aren't some persons who feel that human identity, sexual and otherwise, is not so meager a thing as to be squeezed into some slot and serenely filed away, but only you can say if such persons include you.

Honey, some of you may protest, albeit with a less polite choice of words, *you miss the point.* Butch-femme may be taken seriously, as a mere starting point for more rigorous and varied experimentation, or in fun, as a camp embracing of our heritage while simultaneously bringing a new, ironic spin to the notion that sexuality need be limited at all. *Indeed*, you may exclaim, by displaying our erotic natures so blatantly, it encourages rather than squelches the myriad explorations that constitute sexual practice and identity. Rules, after all, are made to be broken, and the woman who adopts a high-femme drag may, in fact — and as anyone who has ever had sex with a femme can tell you, usually does — promise quite surprising aggressiveness in the boudoir. Many a woman with hair big enough to ignite all of France and too many shades of lipstick to name easily without getting tangled up in the fingers of both hands has lurking within her the seeds of butch behavior, taking charge of the world and any nearby female bodies in it. If we meant it to be in deadly earnest, you may explain — please stop rolling your eyes — we wouldn't call it drag. After all, costumes are made to be removed. Aren't they?

I would be the last person to criticize anyone who achieves genuine sexual and personal satisfaction from life within or employing butch-femme parameters. All sexual

expression, barring that which ends in death or appearances on *Hard Copy*, is a good thing, to be encouraged,
though my tone of voice might lead you to believe otherwise. Anyone who finds something that genuinely pleases
her has every right to stick with it, no matter what opinions other people may have about her behavior. And really,
just because not everyone understands the validity of aping
societal constrictions under the guise of liberating oneself
from them is no reason to assume *you* wouldn't have a good
time doing so. One of the advantages of being homo-
(bi/pan) sexual may be one's ability to transcend the
normative rules society has laid out for one to put on every
morning before going out, it is true, but that's still no reason one should abandon a practice that delights or satisfies
one.

The key phrase here, of course, is finding out whether
indeed it *does* satisfy you, as opposed to merely giving you a
sense of community and self to fill some void better left
unfilled until a more satisfying stuffing may be located and
employed.

There is a bold solution to the entire question, one sure to
challenge and entertain those who find butch-femme
intriguing, and provoke and entertain those who don't.
Instead of a rejection of sexual compartmentalization, I suggest the enforcement of full-service butch-femme. That is,
when wielding the label and its accompanying behaviors,
each person must enact not one but both sides of the equa-
tion. Thus those of you who simulate being butch without
devoting equal time to developing and expressing your com-
plementary femme nature are doing half the job of being

human, and vice versa, though I really would prefer not having to employ the word *vice*.

Human beings, though television does precious little to convey this, are an erratic miasma, a whirling stew of attributes mistakenly assigned the narrow province of either masculine or feminine. Whether you believe me or not, all people have within their pert bodies a combination of qualities both butch and femme. It is the interrelation of warring or contradictory factors that makes life interesting. Consider this: would you prefer to spend an evening with a male heterosexual football player, or a large rear guard whose abilities extend far beyond what normally would be considered fielding goals, perhaps to interior design, styling, and full-body massage? Which holds more appeal romantically, a masculine-appearing female who speaks in gruff monosyllables and brooks no deviation from her strict routine, or a female construction worker whose hobbies include cooking exquisite gourmet (low-calorie) meals, nurturing your budding musical career, and enacting weekly stripteases with your fans, poodles, and wigs?

Truly, the most vital and interesting members of the human race, not including Michael Jackson, are those who recognize and express both sides of their nature. So if you're going to play the game — which I hope you realize you are completely free to do — well, ladies, to paraphrase RuPaul, one of the more breathtakingly well-integrated modern-day examples of butch-femme to date, you'd better work. Longer hours.

CHAPTER SIX

HOW TO CHOOSE A PET

Animal Attraction

It may have crossed your mind, on first glancing at this chapter title, that the author was toying with you. Nothing could be further from the truth.

Owning a pet, as every gay person encumbered by a canine or feline of her own can tell you, is one of the cornerstones of homosexual identity. It isn't clear where the rule of mandatory homosexual pet ownership originated, but throughout the centuries homosexuals have made it a fine tradition to rescue and raise cats, dogs, and creatures – snakes come to mind, but when don't they? – less suited to the obligatory appellations Muffin and Butch. Today the practice is so widespread as to be virtually incontestable. Just as heterosexuals have their own quaint rituals like marriage and the Super Bowl, although the latter is only debatably heterosexual if you think about it, so, too, do we have our lifelong devotion to our cuddly little Snookums that no one understands except us, do they Ookums?

Like venturing into a gay bar for the first time and pretending not to be terrified that everyone will think you're like *them*, like signing the lease for a cheap apartment in a really bad neighborhood in a big city with lots of "single" people while your other friends from college are moving to the suburbs, choosing an animal of one's own is a rite of passage confirming one's entry into a vast, welcoming, expensive club.

Female homosexuals have a particular strong history in this area; some women will find themselves without girl-friends from time to time, but it is the rare lesbian who finds herself without at least one nonhuman family member, whether in addition to or in place of a spousal equivalent and children from a previous marriage.

In the old days, lesbians possessed cats in multiples of two or more, either related to each other by blood or to their owner by ex-girlfriend. Occasionally, they owned large dogs instead of cats, though their girlfriends could often be counted on to complete the connubial circle with felines of their own. Hardy lesbians of old scoffed at those too timid to own both cats and dogs in tandem, not to mention horses and cattle, and the progeny of many prominent Republicans continue to carry on this fine tradition today.

The time-honored ownership of large and muscular or longhaired dogs is still the obvious choice for the modern female homosexual. There are those lesbians who insist on owning frilly little dogs rather than large butch ones, either out of gender confusion or the practical realities of living on a budget, provided the lesbian is female and receives a salary congruent with that fact. She may also possess a girlfriend who is reluctant to share a bed with anything that actually weighs and/or drools more than she does. (This seems only fair, though as anyone who's broken up with her spouse over who just happened to forget to clean the cat box seventeen weeks in a row can tell you, fairness rarely enters the debate concerning intergirlfriend-pet relations.)

Male homosexuals, of course, are strictly prohibited from owning any but tiny bow-wearing canines. The gay man who ignores this edict may think he is saying, "Hey, I'm just a guy like any other guy who hasn't had four thousand penises in his mouth," but the statement he is actually making is purely fashion-related: "I think large dogs go better with my new large muscles." Historically, gay men chose miniature fluffy poodle-dogs because of their portability — nothing says "I need a man" like a beribboned piece of white fluff on a burly arm, pink tongue dangling like an invitation to brunch — and their quintessential yappiness, which converts any male voice to the butchest of basso profundos by comparison.

Many of today's male homosexuals continue to own such creatures, either out of irony, camp, fear of enormous feces, or unavoidable queeniness endemic to their nature. For some reason, few butch females employ teeny dogs for a similar sense of contrast, whether owing to a contempt for accessories or utter certainty of their own masculinity. However, the time-honored ownership of multiple retrievers with hair longer than the entire life span of the owner lesbian's, excluding that brief teenaged shag period, continues to this day.

Meanwhile, the cat thing goes on unchecked. Regulations mandate that all homosexuals should own cats, if only to confirm their traditional status as lonely, isolated, self-involved, eccentric, or friendly, and the incidence of lesbian resistance to this trend is alarmingly low.

Though dogs and cats are the pets of choice among today's homosexuals, flamboyant members of the club may wish to purchase large, exotic tropical birds, which offer few charms to the visiting houseguest, unless you find repeated announcements of previous lovers' names in a loud bird voice enjoyable, not to mention catchy phrases like "I love you!" shrieked continually in a manner even less winning than when the practitioner is human. Those of you considering dating a bird owner, be forewarned: people who dislike the interactive nature of conversation often find great satisfaction in owning a bird. Just thought you should know.

Animal relations: the downside

Though this dark fact of animal ownership is rarely acknowledged, pets can break up more relationships than sex or housekeeping, possibly because both are involved. As any self-respecting lesbian would tell you if only she'd actually condescend to talk with you, animals are standard substitutes for such modern hobbies as turkey basting or blindfolding one's lover's sibling after getting him so inebriated that determination of environs, much less gender of partner in sexual congress, will remain hazy for years to come. Just as children are often the source of much friction within relationships, so, too, are pets likely to provoke jealousy and competitiveness, longing for attention, and feelings of inadequacy or neglect. Unlike children you may share with your partner, however, pets are infrequently the product of either your or your mate's loins, and thus are considerably more likely to provoke arguments and resentment without that handy, ameliorating accompanying guilt.

Sometimes your partner will use your pet as a barometer of your feelings for her, or even as a symbol of the state of your relationship and its prospects for the future. Your girl-friend may believe, for example, that your inability to take in stride her dog's quaint hobby of peeing on your carpets foretells a deep-seated intolerance of her peeing on your carpets, or more metaphorically, a deep-seated ambiva-lence as to whether you will ever really love her. Alternately, she may convince herself that the love you dis-play for your furred beast is a concrete symbol of the love you will never give her, a symbol that grows larger and hairier every week you don't resolve the issue, though by rights there really should be enough love to go around. If you ever bothered to shower your girlfriend with nonstop affection so as to assuage her massive insecurity and enor-mous paranoia regarding anyone ever loving her, you wouldn't be in this mess, though you would be extremely tired.

Every time you turn from a fight with your human mate to lavish affection on your animal one, you are sending a direct message to your human that she is right to envy, resent, and even fear the place – *her* place – the animal has usurped in your life. You are telescoping your preference for someone whose response to being yelled at is rarely to yell back but, instead, to lower her ears and slink off, tail between her legs. As your girlfriend herself rarely behaves in this fashion, though there was that one time after the wedding, she is likely to believe your loyalty to your pet foretells a permanent inability to share yourself wholly and unreservedly with her. Though we know you're not about to give your little one the cold shoulder, it is advisable that you keep your animal love sessions something private between the two of you; you might consider actually pretending your animal isn't around whenever your girlfriend is. The situation with an animal is always easy to rectify, as once you and your beast are alone, Muffin will forget the fact that you ignored her; your girlfriend, however, will not.

There are several key rules to remember so as to avoid the inevitable pet-related blowup. First, never tell your beloved what you really think of her pets, unless of course you love them as completely and mindlessly as she does. By the same token, do not ever ask what she really thinks of your pets, because though you may think you want to know, you do not.

Second, rather than harboring and stockpiling your own resentments of her pets' misbehavior, examine those aspects that truly have the power to derange you and wait until you have emotionally and sexually satisfied your mate to a point at which nothing could threaten her before sharing, in an extremely calm, perhaps self-mocking tone, the fact that you're completely wrong about this and it's only because you adore and trust her so utterly that you can overcome your embarrassment and share this with her, but her Fluffy's tendency to eat your expensive Italian shoes is actually something you feel concern over in the middle of your workday right when you should be thinking about how best to avoid your boss's amorous advances. Confessing her animal's peccadilloes as a quirk in your own character that thankfully you know she's big enough to be able to help you overcome is your only option should you wish to continue happily coexisting with your female human.

The pet-impaired

There are many women and men of the gay persuasion who do not own pets. These brave souls are, as any of them with a clue can tell you, uniformly viewed as suspect in the homosexual world at large. For some reason, the lack of substantiated commitment to a furry child/lover substitute is perceived in the gay community as a lack of commitment to homosexuality in toto, to one's brethren and sistern, as they like to be called. Like heterosexuals who find themselves continually grilled as to whether – that is, when – they intend to have children by that quirky alternative to artificial insemination, the gal's gal who lacks any desire to own pets is seen as somehow questionable, a sort of lesbian aberration.

Often her friends will try to enlist her in the adoption of pitifully neglected or abandoned creatures, as if to reassure themselves their pet-impaired friend is not about to go over to the other side and renounce lesbianism at the first opportunity, which is long past anyway. At the very least, the animal nonowner will find herself called upon for vacation-related tending and feeding of friends' pets. An enthusiastic litany about the adorableness of their little puddle-making companions can go far toward reassuring friends of the sincerity of your commitment to lesbianism, though too enthusiastic a speech will of course encourage the obligatory, "You should get one of your own!" a suggestion/command familiar to childless heterosexual couples.

The only appropriate response to this is: "You've already got the best one(s); any other cat/dog/lemur would be a disappointment by comparison" – a statement even owners of appalling pets seem to have no problem swallowing. Though this sentiment should work as well for girlfriends your non-single friends are pestering you to find, it seems, oddly, to have the opposite effect of escalating the search on "your" behalf.

Name That Pet

The homosexual who adopts, rescues, and/or purchases a pet should recognize, as many homosexuals do not, judging by the pets they regularly display, that the kind of animal one owns, the name one has given that animal, and the method of interaction with that animal says virtually everything about you that a stranger may wish to know, and in fact can reveal volumes about your future potential as a lover, information you may actually prefer to keep sealed.

Perhaps the most common mistake made by your average lesbian is in the choice of name. There are three basic types of moniker available to persons of the sapphic persuasion: traditional, contemporary, and camouflage.

The traditional name says, "I may live in the present day, but I would have been more than delighted to have been homosexual during the days in which life held the promise of secret parties, code names, proper housekeeping in which doilies were prominently featured, and matchmaking only through furtive arrangements by well-meaning bow-tied friends."

Contemporary names say, "I may be incredibly pretentious, but that doesn't seem to bother all the people who think I'm a hot fuck."

Camouflage names say, "I may be walking my dog down a street chiefly patrolled by lesbians, but I'm not one, so I'll thank you not to hassle me. Sir."

TRADITIONAL	CONTEMPORARY	CAMOUFLAGE
Alice B. Toklas	Austen	Amber
Butch	Boyfriend	Bob
Clara	Clarice	Cindy
Del	Dita	Debbie
Eva	Yves	Evelyn
Freda	Uma	Farrah
Gertrude	Girlfriend	Goofy
Harmony	Zöe	Melody
Isadora	Martina	Susie
Judy	Jude	Jewel
Kay	Kitty	Kandy
Lulu	Lola	Lady
Mary	Mare	Marian
Maxwell	Max	Magic
Patience	Chastity	Hope
Queenie	Pansy	King
Rosemary	Sage	Heather
Sappho	Simone	Sally
Toto	Spot	Totie
Virginia	Vita	Vicky
Zelda	Zelda	Zelda

There is a solution to the name dilemma, breathtaking in its simplicity, that you may employ: name your pet after the woman who broke your heart, assuming such a person exists and your current girlfriend knows her name and every other possible salient fact about her. This should keep the relationship you're currently in fresh, ensuring that you will never be at a loss for topics of thought-provoking conversation. Should said heartbreaker not exist, feel free to use the name of your last girlfriend, making certain to keep your list updated. This may, of course, prove confusing to your pet, but a bright animal will be able to keep up with new monthly appellations, particularly if you employ an intensely loving tone whenever you utter each name, taking care to be especially attentive when in the presence of the girlfriend currently in use. Any hostility she may increasingly feel in the company of your pet should be well countered by the increasing devotion you are showering upon it. And after all, isn't the relationship between a girl and her animal the primary one?

CHAPTER SEVEN

HEELING YOUR INNER LESBIAN

The Step Machine: An Inner Workout

Before you determine which if any steps you need to take to heel your inner lesbian, consider these carefully chosen questions:

When I get up in the morning, the first emotion I feel is:
   a.   Elation
   b.   Guilt
   c.   Lust
   d.   Envy
   e.   Hunger

The chief quality I look for in a mate is:
   a.   Kindness
   b.   Intelligence
   c.   Beauty
   d.   Sexual rapacity
   e.   Artistic temperament
   f.   The ability to look right through me as if I'm dirt

My favorite animal is:
   a.   Koala bear
   b.   Porcupine
   c.   Labrador puppy
   d.   Siamese cat
   e.   Squid

If I could wear whatever I wanted every day, I would never take off my:
   a.   Sweatpants
   b.   Lycra bodysuit
   c.   Jeans
   d.   Victoria's Secret special ensemble
   e.   Little black dress
   f.   I would die if I wore the same thing every day

Actually, none of these questions bears any relevance to the considerable amount of work you have to do to make amends with yourself and all the women who have ever squeezed orange juice for you the morning after or of a stray afternoon. Sex need not be involved; the chief issue is the use and/or exploitation of citrus.

Before we get to the Steps (colloquially known as the Trillion Steps, based on their actual number), let's take closer look at some of the ways you do the things you do.

Postcoital Syndrome (PS)

You've met a nice girl. You've gone out, had a few dinners, made out in the lobby of her building, perhaps even made it to the big hurdle and slept together without either of you having to sneak back furtively to the person with whom you're actually involved at the moment.

Now comes the aftermath.

Unlike male homosexuals, who can rely on a mandatory, time-honored tradition of pretending no sexual/emotional connection has taken place – a practice that not only saves on wear and tear but substantially cuts down on the energy one needs to expend (except possibly that used in repressing all thoughts, hopes, and dreams) – you as a female have a number of options available to you.

Ideally, your response after meeting and, oh, *connecting* with someone with whom you have found common ground naked should be comparable to the standard emotions you experience after any physically gratifying/satisfying activity: running five miles, eating a nice meal, finishing a term paper, watching a thrilling movie, writing a boffo best-selling novel. As with these other commendable activities, your response on successful completion of a fulfilling sexual encounter with the female former stranger of your choice should involve contentment and invigoration, a renewed enjoyment of life coupled with a bit of well-earned fatigue. The experience should *not*, though this is a highly controversial theory, entail such emotions as anxiety, wretched unhappiness, insecurity, a sense of imminent failure, and/or dread.

Unfortunately, few women raised in this country actually save their anguish and worry for the things in life that really merit concern, such as their careers (we won't even get into stock portfolios). For reasons that remain largely undiscussed, possibly because they're too depressing to think about, many women channel energy enough to rebuild several small island nations into postcoital syndrome.

To find out whether you suffer from this syndrome, consider, without moving your lips, the following questions:

You've just spent a long evening engaged in animated conversation and eating (food) with a woman you have recently met. After you say good night, do you immediately go home and:

1. Start wondering whether she really liked you at all or was just pretending to like you
2. Tell yourself that even if she did actually like you, she hasn't had a chance to find out what you're really like, and once she does, she won't like you
3. Marvel at how well you got along and wonder whether – make that why – she's lying about being single
4. Go to sleep with a smile on your face

After you and your gal have made delightful, or perhaps blissful, love for hours, parting with an exchange of numbers and mutual declarations of how much you're each looking forward to getting together again, do you promptly:

1. Convince yourself that by the time she gets home (or you do), she'll realize that you tricked her into sleeping with you, promise herself she'll never sleep with you again, and finally overcome that problem she has with saying no

2. Wonder how long it will take you to wreck everything good between you and destroy any possibility of a future together

3. Tell all your friends you've finally found "the one" and start to make plans for your next vacation together, holidays with your family, and finding a place big enough for both of you and her cats

4. Go to sleep with a smile on your face

There's little need for us to stop and analyze the results of this test; we know all too well the number of times you answered any number but 4. The fault is not entirely yours, however. Considering that you're not only probably female but denied the many perks that come with being involved with someone not female, you're doing remarkably well.

Sexual mystery

The external advantages heterosexuals enjoy once they find that special someone hardly need to be explained, particularly to those of us deprived of the chance to enjoy similar benefits. Yet few gay people realize the innate advantage heterosexuals have in the very development of relationships.

Though to the untrained eye the barrier between straight men and women would seem to be a hindrance, it is, ironically, a help. Because males and females have been bestowed a language barrier, whether innate or culturally ingrained, straight couples have an automatic time-lapse period in the progression of their relationships. They may, like many homosexuals, still have sex before they really know one another – for once television sitcoms do not portray life with eerie accuracy – but as nonhomosexuals merrily attempt to build something together – what she considers a relationship and he thinks of as the chance to get laid more consistently with less groundwork – the fact that men and women often cannot or do not understand one another's basic motives and desires provides a considerable passage of time during which they cannot delude themselves that they know or understand everything about one another.

Homosexuals, on the other hand – being essentially the same gender and thus trained to interpret facts and express opinions via what to the outer eye appears to be the same vocabulary – do not have this built-in time-delay period. Some gay men, it is true, try to circumvent the matter by refusing to sleep with someone until considerable time passes, sometimes even waiting so long as the third date in their determination and commitment to finding husband material. Lesbians, needless to say, rarely need to put off sleeping with one another deliberately; even those times they manage to breezily pick up strangers, their conviction that they had totally casual sex rarely survives to the next morning.

A female, even one who has remained fairly nonverbal before getting to know you in the biblical sense, will rarely have any difficulty talking about her feelings, dreams, and past girlfriends once she has taken off her clothes in front of you. Nor will her experiences appear so different from your own, at least not until you put your glasses back on, but she will be too busy assuming that you automatically understand her, and she you, utterly and completely, to notice.

Gone, because of your shared gender and orientation, will be the grace period during which you actually get to know each other as individuals, the way you get to with your many lovely friends. This means the awkward time where you wonder what your lesbian is thinking, because the way her mind works is a mystery to you, is never explored or put into perspective. As far as she's concerned, there is no mystery.

Of course, there is more mystery than any of us would like; no two human beings can instantly know and understand every last thing about each other, no matter how much they have in common. This gives rise to a little recognized conundrum of gay experience. As the ease with which you interact with the person you're dating is little more than skin-deep, by continuing to assume an intimacy you have not earned over time – considerable time – you are virtually guaranteed your relationship will crash and burn.

Still, the situation is not hopeless. Even without fully understanding the roots of your communication dysfunction, some helpful retooling of your modes of expression can go a long way toward a cure.

Express Yourself

From time to time, you may feel the urge, since you have a uterus or perhaps once did, to employ certain timeworn phrases when addressing a woman with whom you find yourself interacting on an in-depth basis, to use a prim euphemism. These sentences, though compelling to speak aloud, can – and inevitably do – have quite a different effect on the person to whom they are blurted out than what you may have intended.

Happily, there are alternative expressions available to you, those times you find yourself in the throes of one of these catchwords or the winsome sentiments attached thereto – alternatives that should drastically reduce the need for weepy 4:00 A.M. phone calls to your friends. Should the urge strike you to express yourself, consider the following.

INSTEAD OF	TRY
What do you want to do the rest of the week?	Great meeting you.
You do want to see me again, don't you?	Is that a 7 – 857-2216? I had a great time. See you.
It took you long enough to call me.	Hey there, you sound as cute as I remember.
But what about *my* needs?	Let's go out for ice cream – want to? And maybe a movie.

It's me, isn't it? You don't find
me attractive anymore.

Would it freak you out if I
called that stripper Sharon
hired for Joannie's birthday?

Man, is that woman hot
or *what*!

Mmm, she's almost as hot as
you, girl.

You're driving me crazy.
I'm going back to men.

I think I'll take a life-drawing
class at the Center. I could
use a new perspective.

I didn't hear the phone ring
all day.

Your mother. She was sorry
to miss you.

Your ex called. *Again*.

No, no messages.

Romantic Fiction

Another human being, particularly one with whom you are physically and/or emotionally involved, has many uses. These should not, however, include the following.

Confirming your worth as a person
Taking away your feelings of inadequacy and shame
Making you feel intelligent, sexy, and worthy of a high-powered job
Making you happy every minute of the day

While she may assist in these matters, the task of fully achieving them essentially belongs to you. Should you expect her, or anyone like her with whom you come into contact either naked or partially clothed, to fulfill these essential duties, you are not only certain to be disappointed but you will over-burden any relationship you attempt to engage in until it crashes through several floors of the building, disintegrating into rubble.

You are not entirely to blame for being startled that these skills are not meant to be provided by others, but rather ones you must supply your very own self. Our entire culture is set up to reinforce the notion that other people exist to give you the worth you are lacking. Everything from music (except when written by Courtney Love) to books and films (except when involving

Anne Rice or Isabelle Adjani, whose oeuvres function as purely cautionary tales) conspires to prove that *you* may not have found someone to make you complete, but everybody else has, so there's clearly something wrong with you.

Happily, once you recognize that by expecting another person to fulfill all these needs for you, you are dooming yourself to a life of continual disappointment, you will do quite nicely living with your lowered expectations. And since you're already quite skilled at blaming yourself (at least those of you traditionally reared on the fun-loving girl program that has proven so rewarding for the psychiatric and pharmaceutical professions), the handy recipient of the blame for your inevitable failure – that is, you – will be already at hand to enjoy the punishments and shame you have devised.

On the brighter side, there are things you may expect from another human being, even a significant other human. A person, even your girlfriend, may not unreasonably be expected to do the following:

Share your enjoyment of life
Make you look at things from a different perspective
Give you support, comfort, or at least advice
Surprise you
Make you laugh
Make you want to have sex
Make you dinner
Give you the occasional massage, though not nearly so often as
when you were first going out

It may seem to you that these options are not dissimilar from the list of Don'ts shown earlier. Wrong. They are so different as to be virtually in another category, which is why in one they're Don'ts and in the other Do's. Supporting, nurturing, aiding, abetting, and helping can certainly be part of your interaction as two separate humans, but they feel completely different when practiced with the intent of rendering whole one seemingly complete but actually radically insecure and needy person.

No one can make you whole, not even – particularly not even – the person whose job you believe this is by virtue of the fact that she's your girlfriend. Losing yourself in someone whom you allow to provide your sense of self-worth is not only addictive but dangerous, unless the person providing the sense of self-worth is you. *You* are less likely to beat yourself black and blue and put yourself in the hospital, cheat on yourself, or scream out insulting things about your body or personality you never realized you didn't like.

Calling All Women

After you've consummated your beautiful act of love, you will want to call your lovely partner in lesbos. As soon as you see a phone, in fact.

Don't.

You will believe she will be happy to hear from you, and that your only reason for calling will be to make sure she knows how glad you are you met her, to provide her with happiness and warm good feelings.

This is a misperception.

You may believe that you don't want anything from her, that you certainly are not calling her out of need (and even if you are, you can keep that need out of your voice and she'll never know). She won't have any idea that the real reason you're calling is because you're female – that is, insecure – and thus are incapable of believing anyone likes you unless you have constant vocal and physical reassurance of that fact; and even then you don't believe it, not really. You tell yourself she will simply think you're being a gentleman, so to speak, a gracious human being who knows how to appreciate the bounties life tosses your way, someone who certainly doesn't take anything for granted.

Lies. All lies.

The fact is, if you truly were thinking about her needs rather than your own, you would not be thinking of phone calls but instead pondering what fabulous little gift you might give her, some token of your affections, serious or silly. A festival of balloons, say, or a nice bouquet of flowers with a card reading, "What was your name again?" Though I may possibly be the only one who would think that was funny. All right, a card reading, "You're too fabulous for words. Only plant life will do."

The operative emotion here is lack of expectation: lightness. Flattery, sure; appreciation, absolutely – but she should not feel necessarily obliged ever to speak with you again. The key word is *obligation*, as opposed to free-floating *anticipation*; otherwise, you will be sliding down the steep incline of mandatory lesbian clinging unto enforced bonding/bed death. In order to succeed in being a happy, healthy woman of the nineties, you must toss out all the ways you've been accustomed to dealing with human relations, also known as sex.

This may seem unduly harsh to you – heartless, even. Every girl likes to hear from the woman she has just experienced nude or any other pleasure with, and anyone who says otherwise doesn't know what she is talking about. Right? All this lightness crap is just that: crap. At least that's what it sounds like you're muttering under your breath.

Bear with me for a few moments.

One of the problems troubling men is that they secretly fear that sex doesn't actually mean anything. This prompts them to do it as often, even compulsively, as humanly possible – considerably more often than seems humanly possible when homosexual males are involved, more power to you, babes. Nature has given men erections to make sure they never forget that nothing lasts, sometimes not even as long as a minute and a half. After love's beautiful completion, they cannot help but feel let down.

A sated woman, by contrast, is happy as a clam: whether energized or calm, blissfully quiet or a chatterbox, the one thing she isn't is bummed out, not until she leaves the place with the bed and is within phoning range. Only when a woman is out of sight of the happy recipient of her sexual largesse will she need to expend every last jot of the energy such largesse stirred up attempting to reassure herself that she didn't make a terrible mistake giving the gift that keeps on giving. Just as men fear relationships will last, women fear their imminent dissolution, pretty much from the moment the postcoital kisses are exchanged. This accounts for the carefree attitude toward sex so many women besides Glenn Close choose to adopt.

The telephone, to get back to where we started, is an instrument that is frequently misused in interpersonal relationships; indeed, it is sometimes the root of intercouple trauma. Remember, if you can, that the phone should be wielded like a vibrator:

1. Gently, paying particular attention to the responses of the phonee,
2. Only when absolutely necessary, so as not to become too dependent on its usage, and
3. Never as a substitute for the real thing face-to-face. Well, almost never.

CHAPTER EIGHT

SOCIAL SKILLS

Things to Do

1.   *Assume people will like you.*

2.   *Expect* not *to fail at anything you put your mind to.*

3.   *Lighten up.*

4.   *Refuse to let completely useless emotions like guilt and shame take refuge and thrive in your body.*

5.   *Ditto self-loathing.*

6.   *Laugh when people insult you.*

7.   *Stop trying to win over those who don't approve of you.*

8.   *Trust that you're worth knowing.*

9.   *Reject nagging insecurity and fear that you're too un/whatever to deserve success and happiness.*

10.   *Stop depending on lovers to make you feel worthy, attractive, smart, or whatever you wish you were.*

11.   *Set a bold example.*

12.   *Realize there's not one thing wrong in experiencing pleasure, even purely sexual pleasure with no other purpose or justification.*

13.   *Risk failure. Making mistakes does not equal failing. Not trying equals failing.*

14.   *Reject passivity, defensiveness, humorlessness.*

15.   *Stop blaming yourself.*

16.   *Stop blaming.*

Artificial Stimulation

You may at some point in your life find yourself out in a social gathering, say a charity function or dance emporium celebrating some fabulous gay milestone, and a pretty woman will approach you who seems to find you absolutely dazzling, irresistible. Or you may be walking down the street and instead of being greeted by a hostile look when you inadvertently smile at a woman, she will smile broadly in response, perhaps even say, "Hi!" as if neither of you had any reason to hide how much you could like each other.

A warning bell may go off in your head. You may think, *This is too good to be true*, followed by, *I can't believe this is happening! This is great!*

You were right the first time.

In our society, unfortunately, we have a thing called "drugs," which can be particularly dangerous when taken by someone you've never met before. Sadly, you, not being the suspicious type, have no way of knowing that the behavior induced while you are in the vicinity of an astoundingly attentive stranger has no basis in reality and will most likely never recur, at least not until the next time she takes whatever it is she took previously. Some of you may recognize this fine tradition from the times when strange drunken women have become abruptly overcome by your attractiveness, but the symptoms of chemically induced happiness tend to be far subtler and more difficult to detect than those that are alcohol-related, unless your abuser is a shy teenaged girl.

Everyone, when viewed under the hazy light of pharmaceutical enhancement, is wonderful. A woman under the influence of the many lovely chemicals available to today's youth will love you immediately and feel no compunction about expressing her love, physically and with utterly convincing sincerity. Conviction, even.

The best thing to do under these circumstances, assuming it is possible it will occur to you to have a modicum of skepticism, which is harder than it sounds when a beautiful woman is leaning on you for a good forty minutes and murmuring into the corner of your mouth, is to enjoy the initial intimacy and try to maintain a somewhat ironic distance from whatever future benefits you can't help feeling it should reap.

Lest you grow alarmed about the dangers modern chemical advances have brought into your life, remember that this is not a new problem, merely a new wrinkle on an old one. Not for nothing is alcohol a mainstay of social activity, both among homosexuals and heterosexuals; as anyone who has ever dated a recovered alcoholic can tell you, it's a lot easier to seduce someone who's in any state other than stone-cold sober. Not to mention sobering, as anyone who has stopped partaking of various substances can testify, to have sex with someone without the aid of ameliorating stimulant/relaxants to smooth out the rough edges and modify the possible flaws of those persons with whom one wishes to interact.

Like moving to Los Angeles, adjusting to the existence of mind-/behavior-altering substances is merely a fact of adult life in these modern times. Behave just as you do when the natives finish your latest screenplay: enjoy the praise, but don't feel the need to believe it an instant past the moment it's uttered.

Coming Out

This is a process so chock-full of fun, it's hard to understand why so many people resist doing it. As everyone knows, the opportunity to show the world who you truly are is essential to the realization of your adult potential, self-esteem, and freedom to behave in a manner most natural to your true character. Why so many people fear doing this when the world assumes who they truly are is the equivalent of a plague of locusts, though easier to remove from the carpeting, remains a mystery.

Clearly, life would be quite different if no one could pretend to be other than who s/he is — if, for instance, any person having homosexual thoughts or experiences would bear some symbol on her left earlobe — say a tasteful likeness of Demi Moore as she appeared in the movie *Ghost*. Not only would remarkably few people turn out to be Demi-free — far fewer than you'd think — those without Demi would end up feeling like the actual minority, and the entire controversy over sexual orientation would become completely moot, except for the ritual abuse of heterosexuals. It's possible, not to play devil's advocate, that should homosexuals with any heterosexual thoughts or experiences — and smooching counts — have a comparable sign on their right earlobes — say a delightful likeness of Bruce Willis as he appeared in the quality film *Death Becomes Her* — a remarkable number of people would have a tastefully matched set.

Human sexuality, if you don't know by now, exists on a continuum, and sexuality itself is a far more mysterious and fluid entity than anyone except the purveyors of cable access have been willing to acknowledge.

Alas, no such markers exist; worse, humans are all too capable of, even skilled at, hiding the penultimate, if not ultimate, facet of their existence.

I myself, not to get too personal, used to eye women as I wandered the streets of a certain urban metropolis that shall remain nameless (take the IRT to Fourteenth Street and turn left), worrying about how they might respond to my frank appreciation. The worst I could imagine – these were women, not teenaged boys – was a contemptuous if pithy "Dyke!" hurled in my face like a cream pie. Yet eventually I came to realize that since this venomous slander was simply the truth, how could its utterance hurt me?

My fears never did come to pass, but I was ready in case they did.

SHE: *What are you, a lesbian?*
ME: *Ooh, you're sharp! What else can you tell about me?*

Alternate:
SHE: *Dyke!*
ME: *Hey, me, too!*

Getting back to you and potential difficulties letting the world know who you are, know that coming out actually offers you a chance to elevate relationships, even simple interactions, out of the realm of the mundane and into the possibly meaningful. Though public perception has over-shadowed this fact, the ball is truly in your court. Circumstances will be what you make of them, because other people, excluding radio talkshow hosts, will follow your lead, taking you as you present yourself.

Should your demeanour proclaim, *I'm a disgusting pervert who does filthy things; everything bad you think of me is too kind a version of what I'm really guilty of*, people will be so kind as to take you at your word. If your attitude conveys, *You may not have met anyone like me before, but believe me, you're going to be glad you did; in fact, glad doesn't even cover it* – well, they will be. Even glowering churchgoing ladies and crusty zealots, though perhaps I should have chosen a more plausible exam-ple, have difficulty resisting the infectious happiness of a gal who wants only to share the good time she's having with those around her. Remember, though, *shared* delight in life's blessings and trials is the key; flaunting the sublime fabu-lousness of your personality in an exclusionary way – gloating, for instance – is not helpful in winning over those predisposed to be wary of the likes of you. Too often com-ing out is a belligerent act when it should be a cheery one, a sharing of pleasure at the giddy roll of your particular dice. Be warm; include others happily in the shining circle of your orbit.

The first order of the day, of course, is to achieve some peace and acceptance from your own worst critic: yourself. You can save yourself years of soul-searching and trauma if you recognize that in being given feelings outside the teeny prescribed norm, you have been granted a reprieve from automatically living a life of deadening conventionality. As a woman, you are particularly lucky to have been steered toward the exit ramp and shown where to step off to escape the narrow bonds of what is expected of women in our society.

Being endowed with homosexual desire gives you the chance to confront, understand, and appreciate who you really are, an opportunity many people never get to realize, particularly female people. By forcing you to face your true self, your nonregulation orientation offers two choices: you can despise what you are and spend the rest of your life trying to live by the arbitrary standard of womanly merit, which places most of its value on such important things as fashion, self-abnegation, agreeability – in which case your life will be a misery. Or you can accept and welcome who you are, in which case you will be free to express all your inner glories without having to be at the mercy of arbitrary and soul-killing conventions. You will be free to do what truly pleases you rather than what is expected of you, and no one will be able to take away what you have come to know and be immodest enough to enjoy about yourself. You may live as you see fit; you will discover that the opinions of others, except your mother, will be abruptly stripped of the power they once had, *you once gave them*, to hurt you.

Reaching the point where other people's opinions cannot destroy the peace you have achieved with your own fabulous self gives you a tremendous advantage, even if you're not normally the kind of person who knows what to do with one of those. Once you are not afraid of being "found out," no one can disgrace or slander you. No one can shame you if you refuse to be ashamed.

Besides, once you let yourself off the hook, you let others off it, too. If you aren't invested in what other people think of you, you become free to enjoy the good in people and let them keep the bad all to themselves. There's really no reason you need it.

How to Reject Someone

As you grow older and increasingly secure about toting the full flower of your womanhood wherever it may take you, you may notice a subtle change in the nature of the problems facing you. Even as you breathe a sigh of relief that you can finally take your shoes off as a woman of the world, you may realize that one of the consequences of entering the territory of the sexually complex adult is this: people will actively want to have sex with you, considerably more than you first realized when you were blithely acclimatizing yourself to strange, exciting new customs of what you realized were your people.

And you won't want to have sex with them.

The fact is, the more self-confident you get, the freer people will feel about expressing their desire for a tender meeting of your souls and other parts. Yet the older (read: more finicky and set in your ways, or else finally aware of what actually excites you) you become, the less often you will want to have sex with them, despite their many fine qualities.

Note: For those of you splitting hairs, we will concede that a greater number of people may have wanted to have sex with you when you were a little more, shall we say, nubile, but as you yourself didn't have even a tiny clue about it at the time, we are invalidating those entries for the purposes of our discussion.

Traditionally, women faced with the sticky situation of having to decline a persistent or unappetizing suitor have felt free to express their feelings with candid, unveiled replies – thus the invention of the word *bitch*.

Many, however, feel it would be a better world for all of us if one could only minimize the suffering incurred by those in the process of being rejected, as who among us save Drew Barrymore and Antonio Banderas cannot appreciate?

In the spirit of increased world harmony, there are several ways of dealing with unwanted requests for sexual congress if and when they occur.

The traditional female way of rejecting someone's sexual advances – and though you'd think lesbians would be excluded from this practice, they by no means are – is to have sex with them anyway.

Though widely practiced, this is a less effective or even desirable method than one might initially think. Chances are, for instance, that if you go ahead and have sex with someone you don't want to have sex with, *you won't actually enjoy it*. Nor does your lack of enjoyment preclude you from having them expect to have sex with you again, try to have sex with you again, or, in fact, initiate a relationship with you that lasts about as many years as all those other relationships you've had with people you were waiting to find yourself waking up one morning finally attracted to.

I'm sure none of this bears any resemblance to your life. I'd like to take this moment to apologize to anyone too offended by the previous paragraph to examine what exactly it is that's got her so worked up.

The best way to respond to the sexual advances of someone with whom you don't actually wish to have sex is, first, to allow yourself to acknowledge your own desires (or lack thereof) as real, and indeed relevant to the matter at hand. This may take practice for many of you, but the more you do it, the easier it becomes. Trust me on this.

Second, you should recognize that while you may find the person putrid either physically or in ways less superficial, there will always be someone who finds that person attractive. Always. Thus you should recognize, even honor, the fact that sexual attraction is a completely irrational thing, a force outside our intentions or control, or why else would there be no one alive unfamiliar with the phrases "alienation of affections," "mental cruelty," or "boss's wife"? Lack of desire for someone has nothing to do with their worth as a human being, their intelligence, kindness, or how good they are with pets and children.

It is far more gracious to offer someone a gentle "Sorry, toss of the dice, babe" than a horrified look, a suppressed laugh, or a smug "You must be joking." You have nothing to feel smug about; you didn't take the brave step of making the pass; you merely had the misfortune to inspire it.

Certain phrases, coupled with a sweetness of delivery, make being turned down a less excruciatingly humiliating experience than women and men the world over have insisted on making it over the centuries. Try some of the following, or invent your own:

1. Sorry. I'm only attracted to women who aren't extremely beautiful.

2. Oh, no thank you. (No further elaboration is necessary.)

3. I wish I did want to, but we can't do anything about chemistry. I'd love to introduce you to a friend of mine, though.

4. Oh, thanks, but you know, I only seem to be able to make things work with women who are really fucked up. (This, like its heterosexual female/homosexual male counterpart, "I'm sorry, I only sleep with men with very small penises," can unfortunately backfire on occasion.)

5. I'd be lucky to have you, but I'm just not very bright, so I'm going to say no.

6. You remind me of my first/last/one true love. I wouldn't put either of us through that again. It just wouldn't be fair.

7. Oh, you can do much better than me. I'd rather not say. No, really, you're better off not knowing why. (This approach may also be used to equal effect in trying to ensnare someone with whom you fervently wish to have sex.)

8. I'm trying to be faithful to Sharon/Julia/Meg – you've probably seen her movies. I shouldn't even be telling you this – she's totally secretive

about us, but you would not believe how jealous she gets! (See above, re ensnarement)

9.   I'm celibate, but hey, good for you! Go get 'em!

10.   You know, you're the first woman I've met who hasn't seemed too afraid that I might – Never mind.

How to Reject Someone II

(AKA HOW TO HAVE SEX: THE AFTERMATH)

There may come a time in your life, unless you're either extremely shy or astonishingly lucky, in which you find yourself having a sexual encounter that does not work out as you had hoped it might.

There are several ways of responding to such a circumstance. You may, as is the traditionally preferred method among lesbians, ignore your disappointment and continue attempting to see the woman in question, ignoring the fact that you are, in fact, not chemically, emotionally, or perhaps geographically suited to each other. Unlike other species of human, your lesbian may well abet you in this approach.

Should she choose *not* to join you in prolonging a doomed relationship, either by failing to return your phone calls or by explicitly explaining her feelings about why you have no future together, you have numerous options available to you: the timeworn method of calling late at night and hanging up without speaking when she or her answering machine responds; driving by her home and watching her get out of cars with other people until you're driven insane; attempting to stab her until she stops dating anyone but you personally, a method we don't actually recommend.

Alternately, you may chalk up the incident to the noble pursuit of that elusive thing called chemistry, the sexual and romantic magic we all seek, and honor – yes, honor – the person who has made you feel that way even fleetingly, even while going on your way. This you can do by treating the person who provoked such emotions in you kindly and sweetly whenever your paths cross, out of respect for the incident and the fact that she made you at least hope to feel a certain way. Ignoring her, cutting her dead when she greets you, or acting as if she is demented to believe she has ever actually met you are not worthy responses to someone who has lavished tender affection on your body — at the very least, whose arms you have felt around you.

The act of trying to consummate an inexplicable, formless desire two people can spark in each other is a lovely one, worthy of a certain veneration and esteem. Such an act aspires to something magical, and the fact that such aspirations cannot always come to fruition in anything more than a fleeting physical encounter does not lessen their value. Whenever two people meet and feel a glimmer of erotic promise for each other, whether they are meeting across a crowded convention room or at two in the morning in a seedy diner, the moment created is thrilling purely in and of itself. Far too many women, believing that sex is meaningless without accompanying vows of commitment, do not allow themselves to recognize and appreciate that sexual conduct is a valid entity purely on its face, or yours. Oddly, this is something few gay men — few men of any stripe — have trouble recognizing.

Many women do not respond well to the aftermath of unfulfilled fantasies: one-night stands that don't pan out to anything relationshipwise. There is, sadly, too little respect given the moment itself — the impulse to connect, the shared dream, the hopeful enactment of that dream, the attempt to make unexpected and inexplicable feelings come alive in someone who is hardly known to you as well as the attempt to prolong them in your own body.

Unfortunately, true communion invariably requires more sophisticated and complex aspects than mute fleshy contact can endow; conversation that is not awkward, but enlivening, can be useful – the ability to connect on some level beside the simply physical. This requires time to know the person, something many women have difficulty accepting once the sexual drawbridge has been lowered.

In dealing with your lesbian, it helps to acknowledge in a calm tone that while you don't regret what you shared, repeating it would do neither of you a service. You may delineate her many wonderful qualities, while gently expressing the ways in which you are unsuited to appreciating them as she deserves to have them appreciated; this does not mean the fault is hers, or yours, or that either of you is scum. Once the pressure of misconceived romantic expectations is removed, you may proceed to get to know your lesbian in a nonsexual manner. You may even find, at some point in the future, that you might be sexually compatible after all.

Or not.

CHAPTER NINE

FAMILY VALUES

Homosexual Insulation

You see them everywhere: homosexuals who appear nearly identical to those with whom they consort, sometimes going so far as to dress identically, confirming the stereotype of vanity and childish self-love with which the homosexual is often tarred – qualities heterosexuals express through their canines and desire to propagate the species – the result being the essential reduction of all humanity to one large clone, a dozen variations on the same essential flavor.

It's hard to combat the impression made by such mono-homosexuals, people who seem so happy in their tiny orbit that they do not desire exposure to any persons who could not be mistaken for themselves. True, many heterosexuals walk a similar path: members of the Christian Right, for instance, and Rush Limbaugh fanatics – excuse me, *fans* – but they tend to be less keenly sartorially matched, and thus at least give the illusion of being different individual human beings rather than duplicates of the original silk-screened model.

The comparison brings us to our point: the ultimate danger of *any* single group or vantage point consorting exclusively with its own kind. To avoid the narrow perspective that is the inevitable by-product of not exercising your mind among ideas and personalities other than your own, you must seek out not only people like you but also ones who are decidedly not.

Homosexuals have a strong motivation for seeking out their own kind, of course: a desire not to be despised, condemned, bashed, murdered, and of course the possibility of perhaps getting to have sex, though this is by no means guaranteed when the homosexuals at hand are female.

Certainly gay women gain a great deal from consorting with people with whom they have things in common, particularly people who have not completely bought into the total female package on sale everywhere. One of the stepping-stones to homo self-actualization is that crucial first entry into an all-female environment. (Heterosexual women may also gain from similar circumstances, but in a less visceral way.) Such an experience enables one to discover that one can be happy to be oneself, as opposed to embarrassed about one's performance thus far, freeing one to be bold and beautiful before one's peers, or at least a wallflower with plenty of equally chickenshit company.

Ultimately, however, a life composed entirely of female homosexuals, or homosexuals of any gender, is not recommended for anyone who wishes to live a multifaceted existence as a functioning member of the entire universe and not simply a subsection of it. Lest you think I'm casting negative aspersions on homosexuals, I should reiterate that the same goes for heterosexuals spending all their time with one another. In a word, do *not*.

The way to avoid the dread disease of monohomosexuality, if the point isn't made by now, is this: consort with heterosexuals. Female and male ones. Consider yourself a friend of not only Dorothy but also Debbie and Doug. All of you are members not of two opposing camps or distinct races but one extended family whose members may need to spend a little more quality time together to understand one another but who will have a considerably better time at Thanksgiving and Christmas if they do.

The benefit of such consorting is twofold:

First, by allowing others quite different from you to share your intimate experiences and opinions, and air their own mistaken and ignorant or at least amusingly naïve ones, you will discover that human beings are really not so different from one another after all. Perhaps more important, or at least more effective toward the pursuit of expanded tolerance and better music at dance clubs everywhere, the heterosexuals in question will realize that homosexuals aren't the horrible monolithic monsters they've been led to believe, or even the witty raconteurs they've come to expect from the Arts and Leisure section of the *New York Times*. Those who don't expect us to be loathsome will learn a few specifics that may even enable them to recommend some lesbians of their own for our enjoyment. One should never reject the opportunity to expand the gene pool, the prospect pool, the pool of raw material, I'm going to stop swimming now, if it's all right with you.

The second advantage in intersexual fraternization is that heterosexuals, not having been inundated with the realities of homosexual life, will mistake your life for an exciting one, since they've never thought about it before, and will inadvertently prove a source of inspiration to the despairing homosexual you've become.

Heterosexuals, when first realizing that gay life need

not be appallingly grim nor gay people pathetic, often leap to the conclusion – erroneous of course, but they don't know that – that the world is filled with millions of incredibly delightful homosexuals whose lives are rife with excitement, opportunity, thrills, and dramatic incident – indeed, that homo life is as a whole exotic and fun far beyond their own mundane, conventional hetero existence. Though misguided, their enthusiasm about your glamorous prospects and boundless options can, in fact, help rejuvenate you to the extent that you're actually willing to go out and give it another shot until reality once more dampens your ardor.

That you may enjoy yourself with the heterosexuals with whom you are sharing your refreshing homo viewpoint can also provide an incidental bonus for each of you: in appearing to be having a good time with someone, you will display your true nature, rather than the uptight, self-conscious one you put up for grabs when searching for love in public places, and thus will attract those persons who are indeed drawn to a lively, outgoing, or at least sociable personality rather than someone grimly holding on to a bottle of beer as if her life depended on it.

As the persons with whom you are bouncily chatting are not your romantic partners, you are free to flirt with those drawn to you without risk of offending anyone, as are your heterosexuals – this is a universal help system intended for use by every orientation, after all – and in the process you all get the opportunity to prove yourselves far less limited than had you attempted to meet Ms. Right in an all-Ms. Right environment.

The sole danger you face, actually, is that your heterosexual may start to behave a little too much like your aunt
Sylvia when she's trying to fix you up with a nice boy.

There are worse fates.

The Homosexual Family

Sisterly love

It may seem, looking strictly on the surface of things (and incidentally because it happens to be true 90 percent of the time) that gay men have it made, at least considerably better than gay women do. A book on how to make male homosexuality easy, for instance, would really require only four or five pages of text; the rest would be pictures, as always.

Undeniably, America's current infatuation with the subject of homosexuality, which is probably just a phase, has by and large given men the lion's share so far, at least where attention, sex, money, publicity, power, confirmation of worth, and societal approval are concerned. In short, though we certainly don't want to be, or look, bitter, when it comes to whatever fun there is to be had, gay males have pretty much been getting the largest slice of what's being dished out in these newly enlightened/alarmingly reactionary times.

Before we indulge our envy to the point of getting ugly, of course, it bears noting that male homosexuals have received the lion's share of one other thing that levels the playing field, especially if one wants to keep score on an eternal basis. Not that there's any need to play Jews and gypsies about health, safety, or success; there's plenty of suffering to go around. Shouldn't it follow that there's enough happiness to go around as well?

What often gets lost in the shuffle regarding the ostensible natural bond between lesbians and gay men is a simple, if clichéd, fact: it is still a man's world, though no one seems nearly as cheerful about it as they used to be, and male homosexuals, if you consider them carefully, are in fact men. Actually, they are first and foremost men, and homosexuals a weak second. Otherwise, they would be known not for instituting a remarkably wide-ranging and efficient system of facilitated, quick, plentiful, gratifying, detachable sex nationwide, but instead for effecting total world harmony through mandatory interpersonal networking, makeovers, and disco.

It has been said that gay men have far more in common with heterosexual men than with lesbians. When it comes down to the gritty truth, the only real dispute heterosexual men have with gay men springs from jealousy as to the plenitude and ease of acquiring blow jobs, and only secondarily matters relating to that other area everyone has but only gay men admit to enjoying.

As long as they can pretend to be butch, a tactic that also works for Sharon Stone and the rare other female actor with a perfect or at least frequently naked body, gay men get to pull up to the bumper and join that club their heterosexual brothers are at the door monitoring enrollment and perks for. Nor is butchness always even mandatory for membership; increasingly these days, unless you happen to live in Fundamentalist country – which in a way, we all do, but let's not open that door or we'll never get it shut – only maleness is a prerequisite for all the benefits pertaining to those with clitoral substitutes, vaginal appendages, or whatever cute names the boys are using for them these days. Meanwhile, even those of us gals whose predelictions render us decidedly outside the conventions of the day are likely to find ourselves still penalized, if you'll pardon the expression, just for being female.

It's easy to be resentful, not that *you* are. Also frustrating about this boys' club is the insular quality that develops among certain spheres of homosexual men, who, unlike their heterosexual counterparts, don't even have to pretend to like women, and in many cases don't – pretend *or* like us. Women rarely have the luxury of being allowed to exist in the world without getting along with men, except on communes requiring Department of Justice protection, but gay men with no use for women are often not in the least hampered by the fact that they wish to surround themselves only with people exactly like them. This does not include "branching out" by socializing with Latino, Asian, or black men as many partial-opportunity white homosexual males so tastefully choose to do. Not that the fetishizing of an entire culture can't be mutual, Ken doll or otherwise. And a very beautiful thing.

Despite the gay men who profess to wish they were female, via such time-honored clichés as, "Men are pigs," "You're so lucky – women are so much less fucked up than men," and the classic, elegant in its simplicity, "I wish I were a lesbian" – sentiments rarely uttered by straight men or gay women – no male homosexual really spends any time thinking about women the moment something nearby catches his peni – fancy.

The trick to handling the disparity in the way male and female homosexuals, as opposed to male and female any-thing else, are treated by the world at large – and it is a trick – is not to make a common female mistake. Don't expend your energy on being bitter, except on special occa-sions in small gatherings of select lesbians. Expend it on getting even, on taking a page from the guidebook of male privilege, on getting *yours*. Don't be jealous of the fact that gay male writers, actors, playwrights, CEOs, film direc-tors, activists, painters, fashion designers, poodle groomers, and movers and shakers get and will continue to get the lion's share of ticket sales and salary enhancements. Simply become more fabulous than the lot of them, so fabulous that everyone will start to wonder and pine for whatever it is they're missing by not being around you.

Complaining about inequities is simply far less effective than writing a dazzling best-selling novel with thinly veiled true-life gay male characterizations, or being so amusing at public events and talk shows that even gay men will be forced to flock to your door to see what the fuss is about. Once you've thanked them sweetly for their patronage, by the way, be sure to throw a party, managing to forget to invite all but a few select male homosexuals, which will only whet the appetites of those you've inadvertently overlooked. Attitude, when sparingly deployed, is an incomparable tool in whip-ping up audience interest, particularly when the audience is male or female.

At any rate, there is a lesson we can learn from our homo-sexual brothers: the presumption of success. Boys, being raised to believe they deserve all the bounties thrust in their path, tend not to be afraid of pursuing those bounties aggressively – except, oddly, where romance is concerned. Girls, who usually catch on early that the most they're going to get from others is a good talking-to, often approach tasks with the conviction that they are certain to fail. Again, the area exempt from this rule is romance, where females exhibit an inexplicable fearlessness bordering on terrorism and a sense of entitlement so unwavering it's scary. Were they only to channel this single-mindedness toward a non-romantic target, the planet would be ruled entirely by women.

And wouldn't that be interesting?

Quality Control

There comes a time in every young homosexual's life in which she will experience her own personal variation on the theme "I hate lesbians/gay men/professional homosexuals." There is an inescapable residue of dismay and shame at being associated with a group that is not only consistently perceived in a highly unattractive way but whose members far too often insist on publicly behaving in such a fashion as to live up to any and all bad press bestowed on them. How is one to feel, for instance, about those among us who choose not to be happy, well-adjusted, appealing members of society but instead make themselves as unsociable, unwelcoming, and unattractive as possible?

Though broaching this topic is a little like joining an already large, ugly mob in kicking a target that's been down too long, pretending all people are equally success- ful and well-integrated members of society doesn't make it true. Just as there is a war among gay men about the degree of effeminacy acceptable in public, so, too, many women feel or at least express dismay at the many female homosexuals not remotely concerned about their lack of social skills and interest in coexisting with people some- what more superficial than themselves. It doesn't help that such f.h.'s, while not particularly eager for helpful dia- logues with flesh-and-blood humans, rarely refuse the opportunity to air their feelings on television so as to enable preconceived unhappy stereotypes of lesbians to live on in the American imagination and to confirm one's mother's worst nightmares about what her wayward daughter has consigned herself to.

Much of our own ungrateful tendency to judge those by whom we ourselves will be judged has to do with our own self-image, what little self-image we're left with after the family unit and society at large are through with us. Most women are wracked with ambivalence about the way they look, mirroring our culture at large, where the importance of outward appearance and sociability is rife with confusion and debate. And what was the point of feminism if not to shine a strobe light on the ways in which our self-worth and actual success are heavily predicated on sexual attractiveness and considerable docility? Other than to make sure slick, self-promoting young women without any sense of history have a target for their venom besides more manly or intimidating targets, who might accuse them of being unfeminine or man-hating, that is.

There is no question that we live in a society that values external appearance, for women so much more than for men that it's almost funny how many gay men would dispute that; so let's just let them go off in a corner and do so, shall we? It's not as if we have to listen to them, unless of course they're our friends, in which case the oral sex rule applies – that is, you're welcome to have your say as long as I have mine, and it doesn't count if you don't really want to listen, if you see my point, which you would if you hadn't put your hands over your eyes when I said "oral sex."

Of course, we all know we spend far too much energy worrying about how we look; the last thing I want to do is encourage anyone to judge others who aren't obsessed with their appearances, though the public representatives I referred to earlier do seem obsessed with theirs, if in a defiantly negative way. Undeniably, people fear those who appear not in any way like them but, rather, like an exaggerated embodiment of some freakish "other." No one would deny that many nonhomosexuals who appear in public or on tabloid television have this same surreal quality, of course; had homosexuals the same option of being portrayed glamorously and regularly on probing, realistic programs produced by Aaron Spelling, we wouldn't need to concern ourselves about every particular face we showed the world. Were there simply more range in the spectrum of inward and outward homosexual personality on regular public display, we might feel freer to join our fellow humans in accepting our own varied role in the circus of humanity.

If more camera-ready homosexuals seized control of public programming, it would quickly become apparent how ludicrous it is to expect one occasional soap-opera character to fully convey the special magic that is homosexual identity. At least six or seven would be required for that job.

Better Homos and Gardens

There's a dilemma that plagues many a self-respecting homosexual adult comfortable with her self and its accompanying sexuality: the question of whether being gay is something incidental to your nature, something you just "happen" to be – or, in the case of practicing homosexuals, do – or something fundamental to making you the divine you you are.

Both of course can be seen as true; on the one hand, you are any number of things, homosexual among them: you're great at macramé, bad at housekeeping, an incredible dancer, good at communicating your feelings verbally and nonverbally. You're blond, at least part of the time. That being gay is one of the things you may "happen" to be is chiefly an issue because everyone around you tends to make it one – somewhat more than the fuss they make over whether you're a good cook or kind to pets. Actually, there are plenty of people making a fuss about the latter, but if we pretend we don't hear them, maybe they'll stop.

There are two schools of thought regarding homosexuality: one, that it is an ordinary feature that should not distinguish us from anyone else – the "we're just like everyone else" argument – and the second, which posits that homosexual orientation radically alters one's place in the world, point of view, indeed entire being. Thus, not only are you *not* just like everyone else, you're proud of being fundamentally different, of casting off the conventions that everyone else feels obliged to follow and hacking out your own unique path in the universe, and no one *but no one* is ever going to get you to shut up about it.

The happy answer to these opposing educational institutions is a cozy little schoolyard somewhere between the two, a place I like to call the "radical mainstream." In the radical mainstream, you, as a nonheterosexual, are a unique, full-fledged participant in the world at large rather than an outcast living on its fringes and making as much noise as possible just out of earshot of the people who really should be hearing you. The neighborhood in which you live is one where you are neither unwelcome nor freakish, nor so very different from your neighbors; a place where you are, in fact, a cherished member of a circumscribed universe your presence actually helps enliven. A universe comprised of people who, given the chance to know you, cannot help but come to appreciate your unique slant on the world once they realize the way you and they chiefly differ is not the sex thing but your view from the edge, your ability to revel in the good things in life and uninhibitedly trash the bad.

Radical mainstream doesn't reject the mainstream; it moves in and redecorates it using homosexual know-how and creative skills, revamping and upgrading its weaker points, highlighting its more colorful ones, though I really shouldn't be using a decorating metaphor, considering what fascists so many homosexuals can be with a color scheme.

Radical mainstream means inhabiting the popular world as if one has a right to be there, which, despite all outward

indications, one does; but it does not require the acceptance of all the rules dictated. Radical mainstreamers are not
consumed with being accepted but, rather, with being
happy.

This is a quality all of us, and not merely the homosexual,
would do well to possess.

Those who don't believe the mainstream has enough to
recommend it to justify working within the system are of
course welcome to their opinions, though I do wish they'd
put them to music.

CHAPTER TEN

HOW TO BE HOMOSEXUAL:
THE CONCLUSION

You're standing at a bus stop. Glancing over your shoulder, you see a stranger walking toward you. She sees you watching and holds your gaze, not looking away. You try to avert your eyes; you do not succeed.

She is getting closer.

She reaches your corner, and stops right beside you. A hint of a smile plays across her lips.

"Been waiting long?" Her voice surprises you.

"Just twenty-six years."

She slides her gaze over you, up, down. Another twitch of the lips suggests but does not fulfill the promise of a smile. Crossing her arms, she looks at her watch, gazes down the street in search of transport, sighs.

"Do you do this kind of thing a lot?" you say. She turns to you. "Travel by bus?"

She opens her mouth. There is a glint in her eye. You wait for her to tell you that this street corner isn't big enough for the two of you; that her mother told her never to talk to strangers. She says, "Shy, aren't you?"

"Only when absolutely necessary."

She studies you as if trying to decide something. You keep your face neutral to assist her in her decision. At last she breaks into a smile, which lights up her face, making her, if possible, more beautiful. Reaching into her purse, she pulls out a pen and paper and writes something. "I'll let you know when it's necessary," she says, handing the paper to you.

You read her name and number. "What do you suggest I do with this?"

She doesn't answer.

You will have to use your imagination.